CREATING THE REST OF YOUR LIFE

An Atlas for Manifesting Success and Excellence
in Life and Work

By
Cathy Hawk
and
Gary Hawk

Published by Brilliance Press
A Division of Brilliance Enterprises, Inc.
324 Main Street
Edmonds, Washington 98020
info@brillianceenterprises.com
www.brilliancenterprises.com

FIRST EDITION

Cover and Interior Design by Think2a
Duvall, Washington 98019
info@think2a.com
www.think2a.com

Illustration by Tracy Daberko

ISBN: 978-0-9768169-1-1

Library of Congress Control Number: 2007933302

Printed in the United States of America

CONTENTS

Part I—Preparing for Departure

Part II—Navigating the Creating Journey Map

ACKNOWLEDGEMENTS

Cathy

I would like to express my deep gratitude collectively to all of the family, friends, clients, and colleagues who listened to my energy talk, traveled the river map, and encouraged me to write this book; making it possible for many more people to live with their "lights-on." As a life long learner and seeker, I am indebted to and honor the wisdom and legacy of the many teachers with whom I have studied, who have shown me that the teacher and the student are mirrors for each other.

From the depth of my being, I express my love and gratitude to everyone who has supported and mentored me through the process of bringing this book into form.

To my beloved parents for teaching me that anything is possible.

To my family who made my growing up years full of rich memories and laughter.

To my sister in heaven, Mary Ellen, who loved me dearly and was always there as a guide walking the way before me.

To Ryan Walker for being the best son I could ever have dreamed of, for opening my heart to a place of unconditional love, and for standing by me and holding the light in the darkest of moments.

To Michael Walker for being a fabulous father to our son, for being my best friend and supporter for the 30 years that we journeyed together, and for being the catalyst for me to go to my destiny.

To the core team—Mindy Mitchell for organizing me for 30 years and transcribing my random thoughts, and Joni Coady for selflessly listening and feeding back my energy.

To Lissa Pohl for seeing the underlying patterns and connecting me to the people that held the clues to my destiny.

To Michael and Justine Toms and the global voice of New Dimensions radio that broadcasts the messages for world change.

Finally, to my beloved husband, Gary Hawk, whose energy informs and inspires each word of this book. He is my true companion and spiritual partner. Entering this book project in mid-stream as a fully supportive and contributing author is testimony to his courage and willingness to co-create a model of empowered partnering.

Gary

During the early stages of our courtship, Cathy mentioned research she had read that said men and women were different in the way they communicated. The research claimed that a woman will use 17,000 words a day, and a man will use less than 3,000. Apparently our acknowledgments are one example of that.

My gratitude list begins with Andrea Wylan who guided me to a spiritual study and understanding that provided me a deeper level of wisdom about how to live my life fully every day. It was this understanding that allowed me to participate with Cathy as a full partner in business and life.

My acknowledgments and gratitude also go to my son, Cory Hawk, who while experiencing and observing the several life changes of his father, has mostly found them to be courageous and somewhat entertaining.

And then there is Cathy. What an amazing experience it is to live with an extraordinary woman who knows that all things are possible, and who, every day, creates the loving space where our dreams can become reality.

Cathy and Gary

We will express a lifetime of gratitude to Barry and Kipra Heermann—whose matchmaking skills are legendary—for insisting that we meet. Our loving partnership began as a wise gleam in their minds, and they saw the powerful energy long before we met.

FOREWORD

Beginning in 1994, Cathy Hawk, as Founding Director of Clarity International®, has developed and perfected an innovative interview and image-feedback process called Lights-On Learning Method™. Her clients see themselves with such clarity that they are rapidly connected to their purpose with intentional, sustainable action.

We first encountered Cathy Hawk in December 1998 in Sausalito, CA when we personally experienced the Lights-On Learning Method™. Michael recalls being stunned by seeing the "before" visuals of his face and then seeing the "after" visuals. The experience was so remarkable that he was catalyzed into a new cycle of his life. He recalls Cathy asking him the question, "If you had all your druthers, with no obstacles of any kind, what would you do?"

Spontaneously he replied, "I would travel anywhere in the world and talk to anyone I wanted to talk to."

Cathy then asked, "Who would be the first one you would go see?"

Michael instantly replied, "His Holiness the Dalai Lama in Dharamsala, India." Within four weeks of meeting Cathy and having this experience Michael received a phone call inviting both him and Justine to attend a special, invitation only, gathering with the Dalai Lama in Dharamsala. This eventually resulted in a private one-on-one interview with His Holiness in his home plus a great deal more.

Justine has had the good fortune of attending the Creating the Rest of Your Life™ training with Cathy and her team. This ten-day intensive downloaded her with the tools necessary to move to the next level of pursuing her work with greater passion and skill. Cathy's river metaphor made a big impression on her. Justine says, "When I could see the path mapped out like a river, I truly began to understand the flow of my creative endeavor. I could see the rushing river with its eddys, rapid runs, log jams, and even waterfalls." This helped her to understand that passion and enthusiasm are a large part of the creative process, however, one must be vigilant like a river captain, skillfully rafting down the challenging rapids.

It is our experience that being aligned with one's purpose and direction is the energy that gets you into your river, however getting into the river is only the first part of the journey. Once you are in the flow you need a clear map with simple and effective steps to assist you to find answers, create breakthroughs and go into action to stay in connection with your passion and vitality.

Through Cathy's years as a vision coach and teacher, while listening to hundreds of people as they journeyed to make their dreams come true, this image of a river kept appearing to her. She could visualize where the people were on the river and where they needed to go next. It was such a clear and strong image that she began to sketch it out on a very long piece of paper that stretched around the walls of her office. She found there were places on the river that every person encountered. Clear patterns began to emerge. She re-drew it over and over until all of the places on the river had been included.

When Cathy began to show the map to people during their coaching sessions, they got very excited. They could easily locate where they were on the Creating Journey Map and discover what was up ahead. The more she showed the roughly sketched map to people, the more they loved it. They asked for copies of their own so that they could navigate themselves when they felt like they were drifting off course or feeling lost.

As people began using the map they noticed their lights-on energy and the lights-on energy in others, and quickly generated more energy and more passion. They spent more and more time asking questions about their purpose in life, what they loved to do, and how they could earn a living doing what they love. Many of Cathy's clients said that it had been years since they were encour-aged to focus on what they love. It became obvious that if they didn't ask daily "what lights me up?", they weren't going to get an answer. Cathy then real-ized how important it was for people to have the Creating Journey Map. They needed a visual guidance system to follow as they quested for the next leg of their journey, one that created lights-on flow and vibrant energy.

We're very appreciative that Cathy Hawk has taken the time out from her many trainings to share her valuable insights and principles in book form making this wisdom available to everyone.

The guidance system contained within this Creating Atlas will help you answer such questions as: What's next? What can I do to get more vitality in my life? What is my purpose, my calling? When I feel lost, where do I go? As well as finding and following your lights-on flow, it will give you tools and strategies that will have you doing more of what you love and less of what you don't love.

Simply put, you have to continually ask the question "what lights me up?" to get the accurate answers about your passion, and to know the next step on your journey. From our experience it's an exciting and lifelong learning process. This book will help you get there.

Justine & Michael Toms
Co-founders, New Dimensions World Broadcasting Network
*Co-authors, **True Work—Doing What You Love and Loving What You Do***

YOUR JOURNEY BEGINS

Do you have the normal human condition called destiny amnesia? The symptoms of this condition dictate that when you are born you forget your destiny. And yet, as you move through your life, you have a deep and innate knowing that it is critically important for you to wake up and remember this destiny. You are certain that you are a seeker on a journey. You know that you are being shown clues, but you are baffled as to which ones to follow. You notice that when you follow some clues they produce a physiological response that energizes you. Likewise, other clues seem to produce effort and drain your energy.

As you begin to recognize and connect the energizing clues, a picture emerges and the process of remembering begins. This remembering feels passionate and purposeful. You know that you are tapping into the answers because you feel guided and your energy becomes boundless. You feel vibrant and alive. You feel like you have come home to yourself. You are calmly energized. You have awakened and broken the spell of destiny amnesia. No longer are you an accidental tourist in your own life. You are intentional, clear and awake as you continue to journey to your destiny.

People who have fully lived a life of self-actualization always report that they never lost sight of their dream. They continued to adjust their strategy by altering timing or financing until they were able to see their dream come true.

"Was I dreaming?" Or "I must have been dreaming!" We have heard these phrases many times as our clients have begun the process of moving in the direction of their vision. Our reply is, "Well, yes, actually you were dreaming." Because the way that a vision comes to you is through the process of dreaming about what you truly want in your life.

The process of taking a dream into action is what this book is about. It is critically important that you stay in the place of your vision – what you want, getting crystal clear about it, making certain that it energizes you. The how-to accomplish it will come in much more effectively at the point where the vision is very clear. Having a clear vision of what you want will keep you from getting knocked out of your game by well-meaning advice, opinion and doubt.

Our purpose in writing the Creating Atlas is to provide you with a guided remedy for destiny amnesia; a step-by-step solution to take you from aimless wondering and wandering to an accelerated journey to your destiny.

Clearly, we live in a vibrating, pulsating, electric and energetic world. Physical, biological and chemical sciences have already shown that everything on our planet has some kind of energy in and around it.

Energy in the human system is the invisible force that creates vitality. Energy's invisibility has made it difficult to describe and harder to discuss. To be conversant about human energy it has been necessary to create a unique language. You may be familiar with some of the different names for energy like chi, prana, élan vital, life force, and doshas. The term biofield has been well established to simplify matters. Biofield is defined as an ensemble or matrix of different energies that extend outward from each person's body.

Establishing the term biofield allowed a conversation about energy to be integrated into everyday conversation. Although energy itself is invisible, the effect of energy in the human system is very visible and appears as lights-on or lights-off. Lights-on looks like a twinkle in the eye, a spring in the step or a glow around a person. The effect is lights-on and balanced. We can say to anybody, anywhere in the world, "That lights you up" and they totally get it. When they hear the words describing what they have been experiencing, they know the feeling, and it's like being energized and timeless. Likewise, less energy in the system is also very visible and appears as lights-off – dullness in the eyes, drooping posture or a feeling of dragging through life and being drained.

Medical science is just beginning to learn that your personal energy field—your biofield—can and does interact with everything around it. Even if you are on purpose you can get your energy drained. That is why it is important to learn about energy fields and how to maintain or hold your own energetic system. You will learn to distinguish energy (enlivening) from drama (draining).

Once you know how to calibrate your energy you will be ready to go into flow. Using the symbol of a sailboat, you will be ready to put your boat into the river and start your journey.

The navigation system operates by your lights-on or lights-off response. Literally, this is how you will guide yourself and make the necessary course corrections. This is your operating system, your human operating system, as represented by the boat metaphor, which will steer you towards your lights.

What floats the boat is an energetic current of flow. And this flow is what will move you as you create meaningful actions, leading you to ever increasing flow, which we call the whoosh effect. The cargo in the boat is your life purpose and that purpose is where your passion lives. Your passion correlates to a cellular knowing of when you are lights-on.

Using the Creating tools, you will cellularly know your lights and navigate from that place. Thus, cellular learning is the ability to discern whether you are either energized or drained by people, places or events. Recognizing when you are energized or drained quickly becomes second nature. And from then on, you can trust that navigating comes from your heart, not your head. Navigating from your heart will actively connect your energy to your purpose.

HOW TO USE THIS HANDBOOK

This handbook is very easy to use. Begin by carefully looking at the whole map on pages 6 - 10 and decide where on the journey you are at this time. There is no right or wrong, or good or bad place to be. What is important is knowing where you are now, and where you want to go. From that journey location, go to the appropriate Principle section and read the Journey notes, and then use the navigational tools at the end of that section to move you to the next place on the river.

CREATING IN ACTION

The first person to use a copy of the map was the 17 year-old son of a client. Cathy had coached him at his parents' request because he was drifting, feeling depressed and making poor choices. Although he was a good student and a gifted athlete, he was unable to decide what to do about college and career choices. Throughout his school years, his next steps had always been clear. Now, with the whole world before him, he felt overwhelmed and paralyzed by indecision. Cathy suggested that he exercise his curiosity muscle, knowing that this curiosity muscle hadn't been exercised in a very long time. A recent middle school survey asked 7th graders what they loved to do. It was astonishing that 90 percent of them couldn't answer that question. Ninety percent of them couldn't remember what lit them up. So, somewhere around age 12, their focus shifted away from questions about what they loved and only 10 percent could remember enough to answer.

The young man needed a vision that energized him to study something he felt passionate about—a vision to guide him.

During the coaching session he successfully found a direction and created action steps that he was passionate about. When the session ended, he asked for a copy of the map to take with him. He hung the Creating Journey Map in his bedroom. He said that seeing the whole journey clearly mapped out in front of him gave him hope when he felt he was getting off course.

By using the lessons and the proven, practical tools contained in this book you will:

> Know what lights you up and discover what's next in your life
> Understand your shadow behavior and how it can stop you
> Link energy to attraction and attract what you want into your life
> Look for the energy lights in yourself and know their impact on living your dreams fully
> Understand how energy shows up in the human system and how to use it as an asset to create powerful relationships
> Remove judgment and criticism from your life
> Understand and use choice points to create your own reality

Cathy Hawk and Gary Hawk
Denver, Colorado—2007

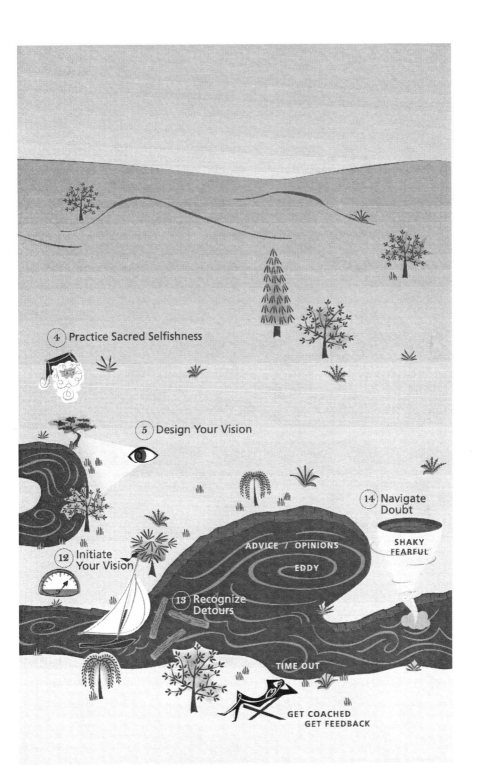

GLOSSARY OF CONCEPTS

Above the Line—A set of focal points that guide you to make choices that are energizing, passionate and solution focused.

Archetypes—Impersonal patterns of influence that are recognizable collectively and individually, and several or more operate during a lifetime. They are like familiar characters which are both ancient and universal.

Biofield/Energy Field—An ensemble or matrix of energies that extend outward from each person's body. The biofield of one person interacts with the biofield of other people and the environment. There is a constant exchange and feedback of information.

Bridge Plan—A method to strategize actions that move you from where you are now to where you want to go. All actions in a bridge plan must be energizing and in service to your vision. The bridge plan actions you choose are clear and intentional, and avoid busy work or accidental waste of your time.

Cellular Learning—Learning that takes place internally, at the cellular level, producing profound physical change. It is the result of following your internal guidance system which senses energy without referring to notes, assessments, or workbooks. It feels like knowing instead of analyzing.

Chakras—Energy centers located in the body that are aligned with the spinal column from the base of the spine base to the crown of the head. They act as conduits through which universal energy and information flows.

There are 7 chakras located in the body and these centers are storehouses and transmitters for energy and information. They function by interacting with the electromagnetic energy field surrounding you and transforming this into the energy that sustains your life.

Location	Relates to
Chakra 1 at the base of the spine	Grounded action
Chakra 2 at the genital area	Creativity
Chakra 3 at the solar plexus	Personal power
Chakra 4 at the heart	Love and passion
Chakra 5 at the throat	Expression
Chakra 6 at the forehead	Vision
Chakra 7 at the crown of the head	Inspired thoughts & ideas

Choice Point—Divergent channels which appear and create an opportunity to choose to go above the line or under the line. Choice points are presented to you constantly on a moment to moment basis. Understanding what to do at a choice point is a key to the process of making decisions that are energizing, when you learn to choose passion over patterns.

Dharma—The "right" behavior from being on-purpose, like being on your path. Hinduism describes dharma as the natural universal laws whose observance enables humans to be contented and happy. Dharma is the moral law combined with spiritual discipline that guides one's life.

Energy—An invisible force/current. In the human body, energy creates the invisible force of vitality, also called life force, chi, prana, élan vital.

Energy Language—A vernacular used to describe the invisible energy that is seen and sensed. It is unique and metaphorical. As an example, the term "that lights you up" is easily understood as a physical feeling.

Energy Patterns—Energy in the human body usually shows up as a cluster that is recognizable as a pattern. Since energy is an invisible force it is easier to see the effects of it in clusters or patterns. These patterns are discernible in the personal field of yourself and the fields of others around you. Examples of energy patterns are archetypes, chakras, light and shadow, and monkey mind.

Energy Scan—A very rapid assessment (approach/avoid) used when encountering an unfamiliar person or environment.

Field of Possibility—An expression stating the belief that all human beings live in an infinite and loving universe where anything is possible, and have free will to choose by changing their focus.

High Noticing—Seeing past words and tuning in to the energetic signals and vitality clues that are constantly being sent.

Law of Attraction—Energy attracts like energy. Your thoughts, words and actions generate a force field of energy, like a vibration, that returns an equal force field. It feels like an effortless movement forward as if being pulled along by some unseen current. Example: An emanation of 7.5 or above on the energy meter will attract to you people, events and circumstances that are equally 7.5 or above. Likewise, an emanation of 5 or less on the energy meter will attract a matching lower energy field.

Lights-off—A dull or glazed appearance of both the eyes and skin, and a sense of low energy and feeling drained.

Lights-on—A noticeable radiance and vitality, with an easily seen twinkle in the eye, an overall glow, and a sense of feeling energized.

Line—The line represents a zone of transition where the choices that you make transform (change) your results (outcomes).

Monkey Mind—A concept rooted in Buddhist teachings. It describes a self-critical aspect of the human mind. It's the inner voice inside our heads that provides a constant, ongoing judgmental chatter filled with criticism and worst-case scenarios.

Near Field—The environment that your personal energy field interacts with daily, like home, family, office, automobile, neighborhood, and community.

Personal Field—The space around your body that extends outward to arm's length. This field constantly shifts and adjusts itself as it receives information (feedback) from the near field.

Personal GPS —Inner guidance, a knowing of what energizes and drains you.

Rapid Discovery—Quickly recognizing draining energy patterns.

Rapid Recovery—Quickly utilizing strategies to regain energy.

Remote Field—The field most distant from you, where world events take place over which you have little or no control.

Shadow and Light Patterns—Light patterns are defined as what lights you up, and gets you into flow. Shadow patterns are defined as what will stop you, by creating inertia. Using a movie metaphor, it is like recognizing your Luke Skywalker tendencies and your Darth Vader tendencies, the light and dark side characters from the movie Star Wars.

Transition Zone—A zone where you are "in between," no longer where you were and not yet where you are going.

Transform—Change shape or form; the process of which involves undoing the present structure and reforming it differently.

Under the Line—A set of focal points that, if chosen, will result in patterns that are draining, melodramatic and problem-focused.

Vision—An image that is clearly seen in the imagination and creates a possibility for the future.

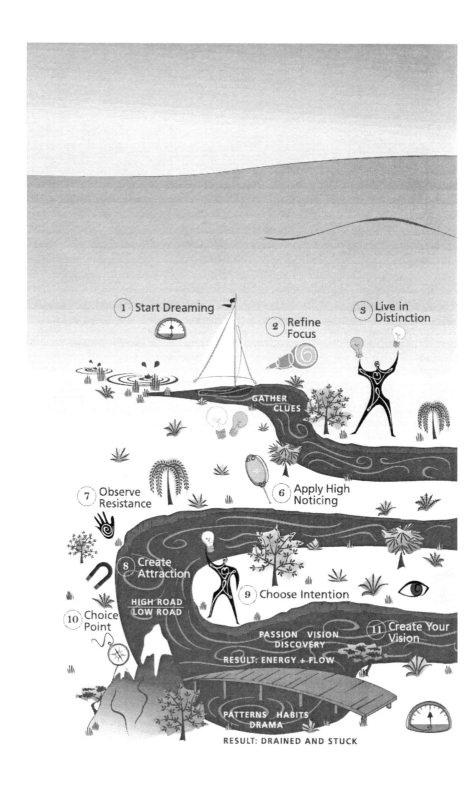

PRINCIPLE 1 START DREAMING

"People are like stained glass windows. They sparkle and shine when the sun is out, but when darkness sets in their true beauty is revealed only if there is a light from within."—Elisabeth Kubler- Ross, Psychiatrist and Author

EMBARK ON YOUR CREATING JOURNEY

This is where the excitement of discovery begins. In a study of people who reported that they were self-actualized and living the life of their dreams, there was one common thread to their stories. Their success had come from staying with their dream regardless of blockages or challenges that occurred. They had all encountered negativity of some kind along their way, from impersonal naysayers to well meaning advice from relatives and friends who focused on what might not work.

Those who truly manifested their vision and lived passionately were the people who decided to stick to their dream, no matter what stumbling blocks they encountered. They listened respectfully to advice; gathered information and facts; and never lost sight of their dream. They returned to their vision refreshed with new facts and made adjustments, if necessary. And they manifested their dream.

The Qualities of a Vision

> A vision is an image that is clearly seen in the imagination and which creates a possibility for the future.
> A vision evolves and changes when it is put into action. This evolutionary quality is a natural part of the process.
> A vision creates transformation - meaning that any structure relating to the vision will change and shift in form.

Actions to Start the Dreaming

On your own

1. Create a quiet space in your mind to dream. Imagine that you are sitting by a country spring that flows with clear, fresh water, or any place that gives you a personal sense of calmness. In this quiet place, start to dream about the changes that you want in your life. It is very important to think way outside any limiting beliefs or negative thinking that you have created for yourself. Be radical and expansive. Go into the field of all possibilities. Spend at least 60 minutes quietly dreaming and exploring this place where everything and anything is possible. It is also critical that you stay in the vision place of what you want to create, and not get sidetracked thinking of how you will make it happen. All action steps will come in right time.

2. Be prepared to write down everything that you remember as you come out of this ethereal, dreamy state. Write down every word and detail, even if it seems wild or crazy. Trust that the wild and crazy thoughts will be connected as you move forward on your journey.

3. Use these notes to guide yourself into the next step of the Creating Journey Map.

With Others

1. Use peer coaching as described below, by gathering two friends who are curious and interested in finding some clues about energy, thus forming a feedback group. When choosing your feedback group, it is important that you choose people who are willing to suspend projection of what they think you should do (judgment, criticism, advice, opinions). We call the feedback group "strategic allies," because they are excellent observers. They can listen with curiosity and look for your lights-on energy during the process without any preconceived notions. Screen carefully as most people want to give "friendly advice." Although well-meaning, people often use their own fear and worry to "pro-

tect" you, which keeps you from clearly articulating your vision. Once you have assembled your allies, allow 90 minutes for completion.

The peer coaching process involves three roles: the client, the coach, and the scribe. Each person will spend 30 minutes in each role, learning the skills associated with each position. The scribe will gain skills of deep listening, the coach will practice pure curiosity, and the client will learn to answer questions as if anything is possible. At the end of the process, all three of you will have your own list of lights-on clues.

Seat yourselves comfortably in a triad, making sure that it is easy to see and hear each other. Each pick a starting role and take note of the time. The coach will begin the interview with the "Santa Claus" question, the client will answer, and the scribe will take notes of lights-on responses only, using the clients own words. Spend 25 minutes interviewing, have the scribe read back the notes for 5 minutes, and then switch roles. Repeat this process two more times until each one of you has experienced the three roles.

The "Santa Claus" question is asked like this: "If I were Santa Claus, and you could have anything you wanted, what would it be?" To avoid leading the client, it is important that you start with this wide open question. When the client answers, look for what lights the person up as a starting point, and continue your questioning by following their lights on energy. If the coach remains dedicated to staying neutral and curious and observing, the clues to lights on energy will be apparent. Make sure the scribe records the client's lights on responses verbatim without elaborating or editorializing.

Expect conceptual answers from the client such as wanting freedom or peace, and then ask what that looks like. Stay curious and question until specifics and clarity emerge.

If the answer is "everything," ask what everything looks like. It is important the client becomes focused. If the answers are "I don't know," just continue to stay curious and playful, and ask the "Santa Claus" question again.

2. The client will then use the scribe's notes of the lights-on clues as a guide into the first step of the Creating Journey Map.

PEER COACHING TRIAD

Procedure
(Switch roles every 30 minutes)

General Peer Coaching Guidelines
No nodding. Hold a still field. No agreement. Stay curious.

Client
Answers as if anything is possible!

Coach

Scribe

> *Asks questions.*
> *Uses interview guidelines.*
> *Uses "Santa Claus" questions from the clients' area of focus.*
> *Follows lights.*
> *Acts as a High Noticer.*

> *Uses the client notebook to scribe "what lights the client up!"*
> *Refrains from talking.*
> *Acts as a Deep Listener.*
> *Reads "lights on" list back with no editorializing.*

PEER COACHING GUIDELINES

While in the role of coach, follow these guidelines:

Never ask why. Why requires justification. Stay with who, what, when, where questions.

Brainstorm with care. It can become thinly disguised advising.

Advising sounds like:
"You should..."
"I think..."
"That won't work..."
"Well, if you want my opinion..."
"You know what would be good is..."

Move quickly out of any storytelling by the client, and go to solution. Guide the client to saying what he or she wants, not talking about what he or she doesn't want.

Hold your own field by staying curious and in observation.

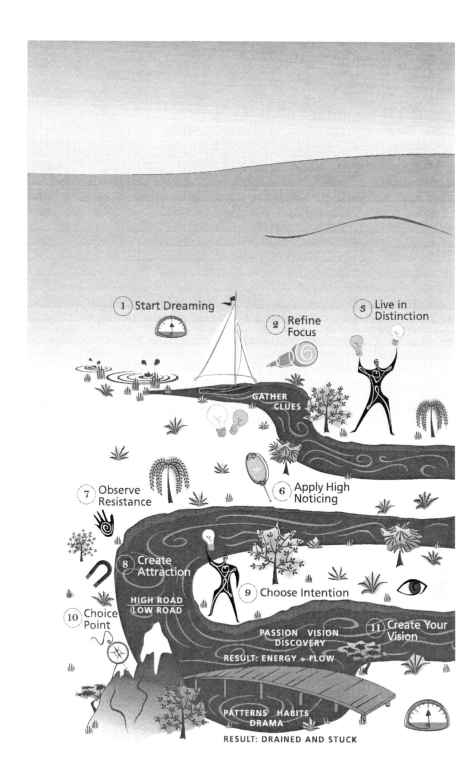

PRINCIPLE 2 REFINE FOCUS

"There is a vitality, a life-force, an energy, a quickening that is translated through you into action, and because there is only one of you in all of time, this expression is unique and if you block it, it will never exist through any medium and will be lost …the world will not have it. It is not your business to determine how good it is, nor how valuable, nor how it compares with other expressions…it is your business to keep it yours, clearly and directly, to keep the channel open."—Martha Graham, Dancer and Choreographer

Journey Notes

> What you focus on expands. You create your own reality with your focus. Your attention goes where your thoughts go. Your attention directs your focus, which leads back to "what you focus on ex pands."

> When you begin to focus on the people and things that light you up, your energy will increase.

> Cultivating your pure curiosity will assist you to refine your focus. Start the curiosity process by making no assumptions, use your intuition instead of your analytical skills; act as an impartial observer.

Creating in Action

Bob is an engineer working in an upper level management position at a large mill in his hometown. He enjoys the team work with his colleagues and the financial security and health benefits that the job provides. It allows him to comfortably live and work near the wilderness that he and his wife, Karen, love so much.

Over time, as the managerial load became heavier, Bob noticed that it was harder and harder to feel excited about going to work. He couldn't see a way out of the dilemma of needing a salary from a job that no longer fulfilled him. Feeling drained, depressed and trapped, he said that he couldn't see "any light at the end of the tunnel" with his work.

Bob and Karen bought a cabin on a nearby lake for weekends, hoping that those retreats would re-energize him. He focused on being outdoors in every season—hiking and river rafting in the summer and back country skiing in the winter. He began taking small groups of friends with him, acting as the groups' informal guide.

He and his friends loved the experiences, and Bob came to realize that these outings were providing his main source of enjoyment and fulfillment. He lived for the weekends, and dreamed of turning his hobby into a full-time job. It seemed like a fantasy that could never come true, so he stopped focusing on that possibility. He gave up, dreaded going to work on Monday mornings, and became more depressed and sad.

Karen was worried about Bob and lovingly suggested that he get some coaching. At her urging, he signed up for Clarity International's® workshop retreat—*Creating the Rest of Your Life!*™

When Bob was interviewed in the workshop everyone could clearly see that he was lights-on when he talked about being outdoors, acting as a guide and taking people on adventures into pristine wilderness. He realized that he was creating a deeply moving experience for people that enriched and transformed them. Although guiding had started as a hobby, the lights-on clues were obviously leading him towards turning it into a business.

After the workshop, Bob decided to focus on developing a guide business, and created an action plan that totally focused on the action steps that lit him up.

Looking at the big picture, Bob needed to stay in his salaried position for at least five more years, even though it was draining his energy. To balance this, he created a plan to get more energy into his life in all other areas. He started visioning once-a-month adventures. In the winter he led trips to back country powder skiing and in the summer he did river rafting and sea kayaking. He began to invite more friends to join him, putting together the groups, getting necessary permits, and updating his equipment.

Friends and "friends of the friends" called and signed up and, before long, he had all of the people he could handle. twelve times during that first year he did what he loved while staying at his regular job; continuing to receive his salary and benefits. His feelings of depression lifted, and he felt lighter and more energized. *As he began to focus on the people and things that lit him up, his energy increased.*

What he focused on expanded. Now, five years later, Bob has turned his love of the outdoors into a viable side business. He has an energizing business that is producing income. Using vacation days from his full-time job, he was able to expand his weekends into outdoor adventures for both he and his clients. He says that this was made possible when he stopped assuming that he was stuck at work, stopped analyzing the situation and "thinking it to death," got curious about observing when he felt lights-on, and focused his thoughts and actions differently.

Bob cultivated his pure curiosity, which assisted him to refine his focus. He stopped making the assumption that something was impossible, used his intuition instead of his analytic skills, and acted as an impartial observer to gather clues and get direction. Doing this has also created opportunities for Bob to do work in his primary job that energizes him.

Navigational Tools

1. Take a 24-hour period of time and become an energy detective. Be aware and observant throughout your day. The less you think you know about someone or something, and the more you notice without the filter of your opinion, the more you will be miraculously shown. There are all kinds of wonderful mysteries out there and you will fail to recognize the mystery factor by thinking you already know. Take the analysis piece out of it. Pay attention to what your intuition is showing you and what you are noticing.

Gather clues by noting which interactions energize you, and which ones drain you. Pay very close attention to your energy. Ask two questions during every interaction and action:

Am I more alive = more energized = lights-on?

OR

Am I more dulled = more drained = lights-off?

2. Make a list of your interactions and actions for the last 24 hours. Use the Energy Meter to rate them. Write down your ratings, as you will use them in the next exercise.

3. Be energized. Get your own lights-on. Then go into action doing more from your lights-on list. By the simple action of leading yourself with your lights-on language, you will naturally be going in that direction.

APPROACH VERSUS AVOID

Humans are hard-wired to look for light. Early humans communicated by quickly reading the energy signals of every new person or environment. At a distance they would look for dark (danger/avoid) or light (welcoming/approach). These pre-verbal energy signals were perceived by using a process of visual and energetic scanning and then making a survival choice of whether to approach or avoid.

This universal communication system is designed to answer the question: Is there anything unsafe or wrong here? Although ancient in origin, you still use this scanning process today. Regardless of any advance access you have to verbal and printed information, in every new situation you will automatically run the scan to decide whether to approach or avoid. Once safety is assured, you expand your noticing and go to energy detecting—gathering clues and information.

This scan ability is precisely the tool that you are going to use as your primary guide as you begin to make choices for yourself using what we call the Lights-On Learning Method™.

Using the energy meter, you will calibrate your scan to a usable principle of energy by thinking of it as a meter—an energy meter, as pictured below.

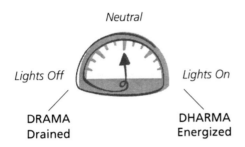

Neutral

Lights Off   Lights On

DRAMA   DHARMA
Drained   Energized

When you calibrate your actions at the low end of the meter, you experience limits, confusion, drama, uncertainty, accidental actions, and you are drained of energy. When you calibrate your actions taken on the high end of the meter, you experience clarity, flow, a full range of possibilities, and you are full of energy. Choices that calibrate at 7.5 on the Energy Meter Scan above are very clearly lights-on. Dharma is the "right" behavior from being on-purpose, like being on your path.

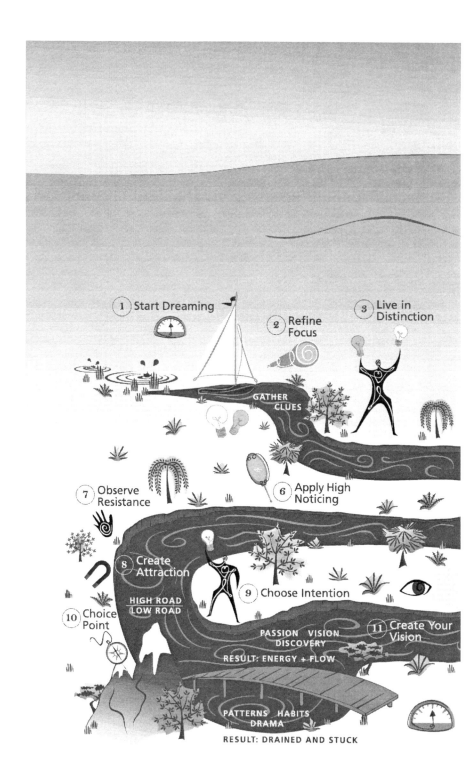

PRINCIPLE 3 LIVE IN DISTINCTION

"A person's life purpose is nothing more than to rediscover, through the detours of art, or love, or passionate work, those one or two images in the presence of which his heart first opened."—Albert Camus, French Writer and Philosopher

Journey Notes

> Distinctions = what's different. Distinctions are made when you ask the question, "What is different?" Accessing the world of distinction is possible if you ask, moment by moment, "Energetically, *what is different right now in my personal field?*" This ability to notice what is different, instead of focusing on the same, old patterns will direct you toward more energy and creativity.

> Space for creativity expands when you ask the different question, "Do I love where I am and what I am doing?" Focusing on that question, kindles the creative spark.

> Give yourself permission to do more of what you love, and less of what you don't love. Delegate the tasks that you don't love.

Creating in Action

Sharon, a successful graphic designer and entrepreneur who is principal of her own business, realized that she was becoming drained even though she was doing the work that she loved. She noticed that she was focusing more and more on holding on to her own energy than she was on being creative.

During the Creating coaching session, she did an Ideal Day exercise. *She noted differences in her energy levels when she shifted her focus from the draining patterns and routines ("same old, same old") and directed her focus toward the more energetic tasks.* Through this method she was able to discern quickly what parts of her work she wanted to keep and what parts she needed help with.

What Sharon discovered as she described her Ideal Day, were two main areas that brought her joy: the freedom of being her own boss and creating beautiful graphic pieces for people. She examined her day by looking at the overall flow pattern. First, she would meet with a client to find out what they wanted and then she went back to her studio to create 5 to 6 preliminary designs. She then packaged these sample designs and met again with the client to see which designs lit them up and to discuss any changes. Back at the studio she would make the necessary changes and a financial estimate of the fees.

Sharon asked herself: Do I love where I am and what I am doing? She realized that all of the scheduling and back and forth travel to the client meetings was tiring and taking hours away from her design work. Being by herself, in the quiet of her studio immersed in the creative process, was what she loved. *So she began to concentrate more on the work she loved, that which lit her up. By doing so, she expanded the space for her creativity to enter; she re-kindled her creative spark.*

The other business processes were critical and still had to be done— just not by Sharon herself. As she became clear about the tasks that drained her, she was able to create a job description that was comprised of everything on her lights-off list.

Sharon was hesitant to hire someone, thinking that if she didn't like a certain task neither would anyone else. Despite these misgivings, she persevered and very quickly found Maggie. Maggie loved the idea of meeting with people, presenting the preliminary designs, coaching the client through the change and choice process, and feeding back all of the information to Sharon.

Even in the beginning, there was much flow and ease and it became clear to both of them to enter into a business partnership. Sharon gave herself permission to do more of what she loved, less of what she didn't love, and delegated the tasks that she didn't love to someone who did.

As a result of following these principles, they've expanded their business, reaching a height that they never imagined as solo-entrepreneurs. They have been listed as one of the top design firms in their city. Working through the Creating process, Sharon went from working alone and lights-off to realizing the work that didn't light her up, to finding someone to delegate to and making a decision to partner with that person.

Both Sharon and Maggie recently decided that neither of them were lights-on about doing the accounting functions. So, at the end of the second year of their partnership, they hired someone for that position. In the beginning it was part-time and now they have a full-time person who handles all of the financial matters.

At the present time, the design process, the client meetings and the financial functions are all being performed by people who love what they do.

Navigational Tools

1. Write the description of your Ideal Day. Where are you living and working? What time do you get up/go to bed? What do you feel like, who is with you, who is helping you, who is on your team (both at home and at work)? Is your energy being drained by any people, places or situations?

2. Make a lights-off task list to help you delegate the things that drain you. Be assured that as much as you don't light up about something, there is someone who loves doing it. Find those people and delegate.

1st delegation _____

2nd delegation _____

ENERGETIC INTERACTIONS

Energy 101

What happens when energy fields contact and connect with each other?

Quantum physics states that human beings are packets of quantum energy constantly exchanging information with the vast quantum field. Whenever you have an interaction with another person or event, there is an energy exchange.
This constant communication and exchange can either vitalize or drain you.

The three basis types of energetic exchanges:
1. **Neutral**—*you have a very surface reaction, no impact on your energy.*
2. **Draining**—*you feel tired and worn out when the interaction is finished.*
3. **Energizing**—*you feel more alive e and awake when the interaction is finished.*

Energizing (positive)	Draining (negative)
Intention	**Intention**
To learn more about someone else and what gives them vitality.	*To tell more about yourself.*
Questions	**Questions**
Who, what, when, where, how.	*"Why"—requires justification.*
True Curiosity	**Imposter Curiosity**
True interest in other person, with-out judgment or criticism.	*Judgment (cloaked as questions) "Why do you always…"*
Acknowledgement	**Advice and Opinion**
"I hear what you are saying…"	*"You should…"*
Alignment	**Agreement**
Don't make the other person wrong. Don't have to agree.	*Convincing. Assumes there is only one right way.*
Supports authenticity, vitality and balance.	Creates resistance, conflict and rigidity.
Chaos (natural state of the universe)	*Confusion*
Intentional (focused)	*Accidental (random)*
Empowered Actions	*Control "freaks"*

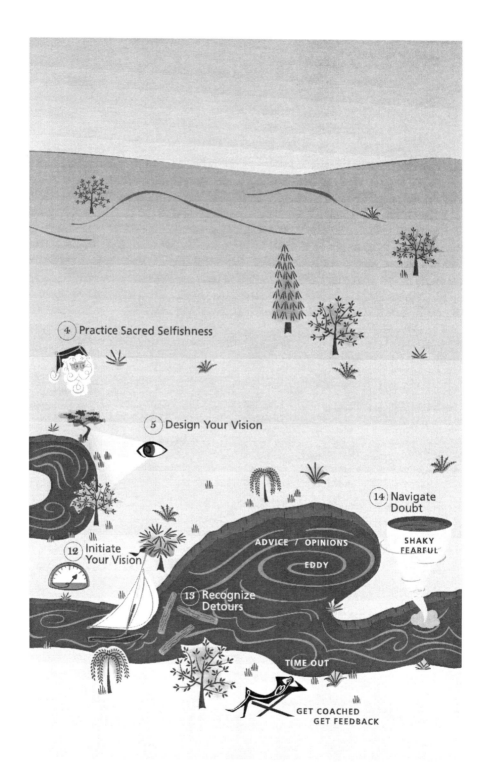

PRINCIPLE 4 PRACTICE SACRED SELFISHNESS

"The Universe has a matching grants fund."—Michael Toms, Founder, New Dimensions Radio

Journey Notes

> Fullness creates possibility and generosity. When you are full and getting everything you want, there is a ripple effect that touches everyone around you. This is defined as holding your personal energy field and this "selfishness" is the quickest way to generosity. Protect yourself from being drained by people and circumstances in your near field. Make sure that your needs are met deeply, and that you have a reserve amount of time, money, love, joy, vitality and creativity. Take the time to discover what lights you up and simply practice being "selfish".

> You must serve yourself and your vision first before focusing on others. You cannot give if your personal energy field is drained and you have be come an empty vessel. It is paradoxical that in order to go to high service, you have to serve yourself first. It is like those in-flight airplane emergency drills; you are told to put the oxygen mask on yourself first in order to stay alive and be of service to others. Sacred selfishness is the quickest way to generosity.

> All things are possible; the only limitations are the ones that you place upon yourself. Limitless, multiple choice thinking creates an energy field full of possibilities. It forms when you fill yourself up versus depleting your self. If you feel yourself going lights-off or losing energy, immediately stop and ask yourself the Santa Claus question: If I can have anything I want, what will that look like? Answer as if anything is possible—be both specific and expansive.

Creating in Action

When Diane entered the Creating the Rest of Your Life™ workshop, she owned a very successful real estate marketing business. Her firm managed the entire sales process for developers as they created and built new housing projects. She gave the developers design ideas that would appeal to buyers; created all of the sales and marketing materials; and hired and managed the entire sales team.

Diane really loved this initial phase of launching a new project. However, she began to notice that even with a lot of staff to help her, she was running herself ragged. That is exactly how she described it. She was going in many different directions, always feeling scattered and ungrounded. There was so much on her plate that she could no longer sort through it all to decide what was really important to her. Basically, everything she was doing really did light her up, and it was also exhausting her.

In a coaching session, Diane went through everything that she was doing daily in both her work and in her life. Each task was assigned a 1-10 rating using the Energy Meter. Since all of her daily tasks lit her up at 7 or above, she had to go to a finer distinction and rated her tasks by BIG lights—9 or above. This process helped her to distinguish what was extremely important to her. It enabled her to remove scatter and distraction from her personal and near fields, and focus her energy and attention. *She discovered that all things were possible; the only limitations are the ones that she placed upon herself.*

The coaching revealed that in addition to loving her work, she also had a philanthropic passion and was in charge of an international non-profit relief project to help refugees. *Fullness creates possibility and generosity.* She was doing her full-time business, managing all the sales people, loving all that and also organizing an overseas not-for-profit. She did have a lot on her plate.

Diane was asked the Santa Claus Question: *If you can have anything you want, what will that look like? What do you want right now in this moment?* She began sorting through all of her daily tasks and activities with the instruction to get "selfish" and clearly choose what really lit her up. It was also important for her to notice that whenever she was getting drained by any of the projects, an equal energetic drain was created within the projects. *When Diane was full and getting everything she wanted, there was a ripple effect which touched everyone around her. Likewise, when she was drained there was a ripple effect which touched everyone around her.* A field of possibility and generosity was formed when she filled herself up versus depleting herself. This was the key: to fill herself first instead of giving her energy away.

It is paradoxical that in order to go to high service, Diane had to serve herself first. Using the principle of Sacred Selfishness, Diane distilled it down to two things that she loved the most: being the visionary for the real estate project and being the visionary for the overseas charity project. She got clear about what was draining her: the continual doing, the running around to obtain donations, and the errands relating to paperwork and administration. To make everything lights-on for her, she hired a detail person to manage each of the projects, worked with them to develop a checklist of tasks, established a feedback loop to receive their reports, and proceeded with the delegation.

She shifted from being a "control freak" to being a "control tower" and this enabled her to perform as the visionary for both of the projects. Both of her new project managers said she was very clear about the parts that she loved and delegated the rest to them.

Because of her clarity and delegation, both of the projects have evolved and doubled their effectiveness and capabilities. *Diane took a long linger in the "what she wanted" (vision), and ignored the "how to do it" (strategy) until she was very clear.* Being very clear about her vision before figuring out how to accomplish it conserved her energy for getting it all done.

By cutting what she was doing in half, the ripple affect in her field doubled the energy on both of the projects. *Fullness created possibility and generosity.*

Navigational Tools

1. Get together with a good friend who promises not to comment and/or give opinions about your answers. Ask them to help you with this exercise by asking—"If I were Santa Claus and you could have anything that you wanted, what would that be?" They will ask that question many times until you run out of subjects. Take a lot of time exploring the "what you want" answers. It is important, during this time, to ignore the "how to do it". If you go to the how (strategy) before you are completely clear about the what (vision), you will deplete your energy, and block the discovery.

2. Ask your friend to be the scribe and write down only lights-on answers.

3. If you catch yourself talking about what you *don't* want, go back and make sure that your scribe writes down every lights-on clue even if they seem random and disconnected. These clues will make sense later when you apply them in your two energy fields: personal and near.

COMPASS POINT 1—ENERGY FIELDS

Holding your own personal energy field is critical to living a passion connected life.

It's easy to get your lights taken out (energy drained) with all that is going on in the world today. Many of us find that we're moping around, anxious, angry, and on edge. This is ideal time to remember and put to use the phrase, "What you focus on expands." If you focus on all that is wrong, you will feel even worse, and your negative energy becomes infectious to all aspects of your life. Instead, it's better to remember that your positive energy can ultimately have a much greater impact on the world by counteracting the negative. The Law of Attraction will bring you more of the energy you create.

To help maintain your own positive energy in all that you do, recognize that there are three energy fields.

The Remote Field—*Distant Energy System*

This is the field most distant from you. It involves events taking place in the world over which you have little or no control. War is an example. Gulf coast hurricane disasters are another example. Even though you are not directly in that field, you are impacted by it. When you let the negative aspects of the remote field consume you, it's like bringing the war and the natural disaster into your home. You can lose your own energy and become lost, anxious and on edge.

The remote field can have an energy draining effect on you, only if you let it. Our culture has a tendency to direct your focus to the remote field. In school your studies were mostly about the remote field, or things that are far away from you. The daily news bombards you with information about war, the ups and downs of the stock market, crime, accidents and danger. By allowing yourself to be affected by this invasion from the remote field, you can become victimized by events that are random and largely out of your control. You can easily allow these events to determine what happens in your personal life and space if you are not mindful or aware of that possibility.

However, your positive energy can ultimately have a great impact on the world by counteracting the negativity in the remote field. There is a popular science idea from chaos theory that an insect fluttering its wings in the Pacific can create hurricanes in the Atlantic. Never underestimate your power to generate change, even from very personal and seemingly small actions.

Examples of Remote Field Energy Language
> "That news piece made my skin crawl."
> "When the stock market goes up I feel like a giant weight has been lifted from me."
> "The polarization of politics in this country angers and depresses me."

Actions to Diminish the Effects of Remote Field Energy
1. Do you let news events bring negativity and fear into your home? Try going to bed without watching the late-night news. Notice if your sleep is more restful or if you wake up with less anxiety.
2. Do you focus on what's wrong in the world? Try listening to positive talk radio and other media which aim to deliver the news without the "alarm" voice tones.
3. Don't listen to or read the news at all, and choose carefully how you receive news you may need or want to know. This doesn't mean ignoring what is going on—it is simply a way to keep from being consumed by the negativity.

The Near Field—*Environmental Energy System*
The near field is your environment—your home, family, neighborhood, office and community. It is the field of energy that your personal energy field interacts with daily. This is your support field. You can't completely control this field; however you do have strong influence over it. You can best affect this field by intentionally choosing your friends, partners and immediate surroundings.

Does your environment enhance your life? Are you living in a home you love? Do you feel soothed when you walk into your home? Do you love your office? Is it clear of clutter, or are there piles of clutter everywhere? What are the qualities of your near environment that support and enliven you?

Are your friends, partners and neighbors supportive of you? Are they energizing to be around, or do you feel drained and tired after spending time with them?

You connect with and interact with your near field continuously. It is critical that you do all you can to have its impact on you be supportive, energizing and enlivening.

Examples of Near Field Energy Language

> "Every time I talk with her, I leave feeling angry and frustrated."

> "He lights up the whole room."

> "The pressures of my day disappear as soon as I walk in my front door."

Actions to Enhance Your Near Field Energy

Ask yourself the following questions and give the answers a rating of 1 – 10 from the energy meter.

1. Does my environment enhance my life? _____

2. Do I feel soothed when I walk into my home and office? _____

3. Do my friends, partners, and neighbors support me? _____

Note that any answer that rated 5 or below is an area to be changed. Go into action to make the necessary changes. If your home or office is cluttered, de-clutter it. If your friends are draining your energy, re-evaluate the friendship, or let them know how they can be supportive.

Your Personal Field—*Human Energy System*

"Like other kinds of energy fields, the human energy field is stronger at its source and fades with distance. In this regard, it behaves similarly to other fields recognized in physics. No doubt you can think of people you know who seem to radiate stronger energy than others, as if their energy field is somehow bigger or more potent. In fact, we have many expressions in our language for this, such as when we describe an unusually radiant or high energy person. Another way our personal field is like oth-

er fields in nature is that it has qualities of polarity: positive and negative, north and south."—William Collinge, Subtle Energy

The primary tool to achieving your life's destiny is to hold your personal energy field in all circumstances. Your personal energy field is your body and the arm's length space around you—your health, your thoughts, your nutrition, your sleep and your spirit.

You have total control over your personal energy field. A major focus of this book is about is understanding how you control this field, and hold your own energy, no matter what is happening around you. What is it that you can do to stay alive and conscious and lights-on? The body, mind and spirit of your own energy field are very controllable through the daily, moment by moment choices you make.

Examples of Personal Field Energy Language
> "I woke up on the wrong side of the bed."
> "I am healthy. I do healthy things with my body."
> "Today is going to be a great day."
> "I wonder what other people think of me?"

Actions to Enhance Your Personal Energy Field
1. When feeling the negative energy from the remote or near fields, ask yourself what good you will do if you are consumed by anger, fear and despair.
2. To keep your own lights on during difficult times, concentrate on what you love. It helps to create a personal mantra or intention to stay strong and focus on solutions rather than fear.
3. You can also listen to beautiful music, maintain regular exercise, eat healthy food, and practice self-care rituals. Above all, remind yourself to send out as much positive energy as possible, in order to counteract all the negativity in the remote field.

THE THREE ENERGY FIELDS

Personal Field	• Your body and the space around you (arm's length) • Your health, nutrition, sleep, thoughts, and spirit • The combination of body/mind/spirit • You can have total control through your choices (attention and intention and actions)
Near Field	• Your environment: partners, children, family, pets, vehicles, work place/office • You can have a lot of control over this field, and can influence outcomes
Remote Field	• Distant to you; It can be anything from the other side of the city to the other side of the world • TV, newspapers, radio, internet, external input • You have very little control over this field

In Summary

Basically: *personal* is **you**; *near* is your **environment**; and *remote* is the **whole world**. The importance of understanding energy fields is that you are affected by all of the fields only to the extent that you allow it to happen. For example, you really don't have control over the remote field; however, you do have control over how you let it affect you through the conscious use of your language. Since language helps to create your reality, use "energy talk" as much as you can by speaking in a way that accurately describes the energy that you are seeing or sensing—in yourself, in others around you and in places and situations. Avoid saying things like: "It kills me to hear about that," or "I cry every time that I see that image," or "I am so angry at (or afraid of) what is happening in the world."

This simple practice of speaking an energetic language, such as "that lights me up" or "that knocks my lights out" will shift your focus, make you more aware and expand your possibilities to more positive results.

Learning how to hold your own energy, no matter what happens, is a critical step in staying true to your vision.

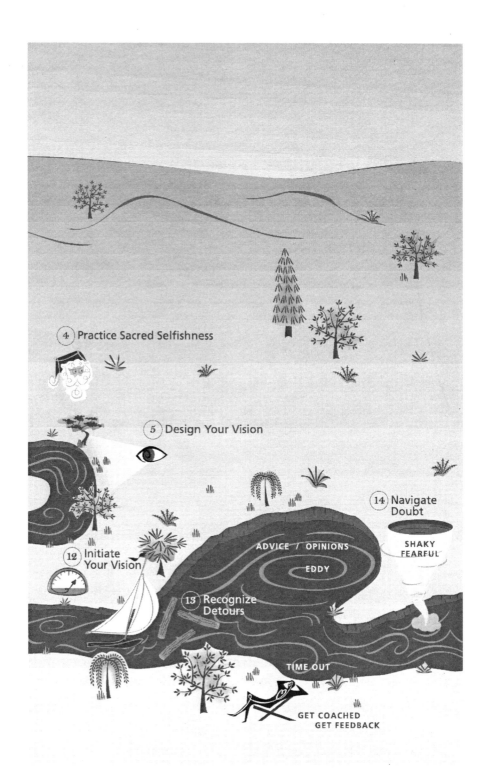

PRINCIPLE 5 DESIGN YOUR VISION

"When master sculptors make figures out of wood or stone, they do not intro-duce the figure into the wood, but chisel away the fragments that concealed the figure; they give nothing to the wood, rather they take away from it, letting fall beneath the chisel the outer layers, removing the rough covering, and then what had lain hidden beneath shines out."—Meister Eckhart, Theologian and Christian Mystic

Journey Notes

> Clutter creates confusion and blocks flow. Clutter is a clue for any-thing in your personal and near fields which drains your energy or creates blockage to your system or surroundings. Designing your vision is as much about removing obstacles as it is about creating and moving forward.

> Confusion and busyness in your field will cloud your vision. Confu-sion enters with overdoing. Anything that calibrates at 5 or below on the Energy Meter will cause you to overdo and become obligated and drained.

> Energy flows where your attention goes, and your focused atten-tion, free of clutter, enables you to create your own reality.

Creating in Action

When Arlene began the Clarity process, she lived in a large home filled with many beautiful objects—collections with meaning and value to her. Within her home was an office that held files and paperwork from her business. She also had a second office outside of her home where she met clients, which held more paper, files and business equipment. Additionally, she had a third loca-tion, which was a weekend beach place. Although all of these places were very orderly and neat, she felt that she was almost paralyzed in her life.

The realization that her collections felt like too much "stuff"—or clutter—was a big clue as to what was draining her energy and creating a blockage in her ability to move forward with ease and clarity.

Between the three places, Arlene spent a lot of time searching for things. This unproductive and aimless use of her time drained her. *Confusion and busyness in her field clouded her vision.* As a result, she felt totally scattered and unable to decide where or what she wanted to do next. She couldn't decide how to go forward, and she felt overwhelmed all of the time. *It became clear to Arlene that clutter was creating her confusion and lack of flow.*

Her first step was to begin to clear the clutter. Using the Energy Meter concept, she noted everything in her spaces that calibrated energetically at 7 or below.

Arlene began with her outside office by walking through it and noticing that it did not light her up. On the contrary, it drained her. She decided to get rid of that property and down-size into one office space. This task seemed so overwhelming that she hired a professional organizer to assist her with the process. The organizer helped her sort, systematize and consolidate everything into her home office. Now, when she went into the one office she could find things easily and she enjoyed being there. Arlene immediately began to feel clear, focused and energized.

After a year of feeling very grounded and on purpose, Arlene decided that traveling between her house and the beach house wasn't lighting her up anymore. She felt she was always in limbo and never really present in one place or the other. She made the decision to sell the beach house.

Again, she brought in the professional organizer to help her downsize. She picked only the things that she loved from the beach house and brought those things back to the main house. In doing that, she began to feel very stuck and overwhelmed by everything that was stored in the main house. So, Arlene went through another process of clearing, which included donating clothing to charity that she no longer enjoyed wearing. It took about a year to sort through, downsize, consolidate and clear her home. She noticed that she felt very present. She could walk into her home and into her home office and be focused, directed and able to go to business.

This new level of clarity lasted for about a year. Arlene decided she wanted to downsize once again in order to gain the freedom to travel more. She literally went through each and every object in her house. An assistant walked with her, took notes of 7+ energy rating on everything and Arlene kept only the things that truly lit her up. All the rest of her belongings were either donated or sold.

She was also clear about the fact that maintaining property was not lighting her up. She decided to sell her house and move into a high rise condominium where the maintenance was handled by others. Arlene moved into a very spacious condominium and in it were only the things she loved, including her own office. ***Energy flows where your attention goes.***

Now both Arlene's life and business have flow. She lives and works with clarity and ease in a very clear field surrounded by everything that lights her up.

Navigational Tools

1. Scan your fields using the Energy Meter principle. Make notes of anything that registers 7 or above. This will become a part of the vision of your Ideal Day.

2. Using the clues from Principle 3—your Ideal Day—design your vision as a virtual experience of your Ideal Day, this allows you to verify whether you are lights-on or lights-off in any given situation.

3. Clear Clutter—remove any items in your personal and near fields that do not support your new vision. Pay attention to what creates flow and what that prevents you from going into flow is defined as "clutter."

4. Never ask why—just notice the reflection of energy.

5. Take a day devoted to experiencing this Ideal Day, looking for synchronicities and clues. Write your experiences in your journal.

COMPASS POINT 2—RITUAL AND CHECK-IN

Using a Personal Ritual and Check-in to Hold Your Own Field

There is a lot of drama being modeled in our culture at this time, especially in the media. This results in you being exposed daily to more drama and melodrama than ever before. It is easy to fall into the trap of confusing drama and energy. The key distinction between the two is that drama will drain you, and energy will enliven you.

To avoid draining interactions, focus on holding your own energy during all exchanges. As you continue to develop this critical skill, you will notice your personal field becoming steady and strong. With experience you will rarely feel drained, and the energy vampires will have to go elsewhere to get their juice. This is the essence of rapid discovery and rapid recovery.

Staying focused and intentional requires being conscious and aware every day—about holding your energy and keeping true to your vision. Learning how to consistently hold your own personal energy field is the most important element of creating the life you want to live.

There are two key strategies to assist you in developing and sustaining a strong and intentional personal field—using a daily personal ritual and a daily check-in.

Personal Ritual

A ritual is a personal energy tool that assists you in setting and holding your personal field and the near field. It can ground you, connect you to your intentions, free you from the emotions of your ego, and anchor the way you approach your daily interactions. When you use your own personal ritual, you are choosing to live intentionally, with clarity and compassion. Personal rituals are found in every culture around the world, and they serve the purpose of disengaging you from any drama in a situation. This lets you become the observer rather than absorber. You will act more like a mirror than a sponge. Your personal ritual sets your personal energy field.

Create your own ritual by starting with the qualities you want in your own field. Make it simple and easy to repeat either out loud or quietly to yourself. You may also find it helpful to ground yourself before you say your ritual. Close your eyes and imagine dropping an imaginary cord to earth's center, hook onto the center, and feel the deep grounding connection you have with the earth. Breathe deeply while both feet are firmly on the ground.

You may also want to use mudras or hand gestures. Mudra is a Sanskrit word meaning seal or sign, used by the yogis in India to describe the ritual hand gestures they practice during meditation. Other spiritual traditions use hand gestures, for example, Christians put palms together while praying and Chinese masters of Qigong put their palms to the heavens to call in universal energy. Any higher quality you aspire to can be sealed and activated with its own mudra.

An example of a personal ritual:

God, Universe, and all other Guides, grant me wisdom, skill, and knowledge to be of highest service to all. Assist me to hold a constant energy field around me at all times where I feel only love, and see only beauty. Let this force field create an attraction for others so I may attract love, joy, connection, community and abundance.

It is very important that your daily ritual be done in a conscious manner. Be conscious of the words you state, feel them in your body, sense how they impact you. When you say "I feel only love" or "I attract joy" let that feeling of love flow through your body, and let the joy be expressed in your face, your smile.

Most importantly let it serve you. Create your ritual to serve yourself, reconnect you to the sacred aspects of your life, and set your energy for the day.

Daily Check-in

The daily check-in is an exercise in learning levels of distinction by answering five questions. The check-in process is completely focused on the self. This is an exercise you can do by your self or with others, and can be done in as little as five minutes. When done alone, it is an internal conversation that will ground you and keep you conscious. This is a very important exercise. It is one of the simplest and most critical elements of the Clarity operating system. It will keep you focused and disciplined.

When the daily check-in is done with another person, it is a very powerful relationship tool that deepens the connection, and offers a method to improve communication and understanding. However, its primary purpose is to keep you focused on your self, and holding your own energy field against the pressures of your monkey mind talk, and the energy drain from others in your near field.

There is a natural tendency to think the state of your personal field is related to another's actions. You are not capable of controlling other's actions. You are only able to control your own field, therefore during the check-in you can never comment on anyone else's behavior.

The five questions of the daily check-in are:

What's different?

What worked and what didn't work?

What is the state of my mind, body and spirit?

What am I grateful for?

What is my intention for today?

What's different?

The first question to ask is "What's Different?" One of the principles of quantum physics is that in every nano-second everything is different. In order to access quantum reality (which is also the physics of all possibilities), it is important to notice that everything is different all the time. Noticing this, and not operating from the place of "same old, same old", wakes you up, keeps you conscious of the differences in your daily life. Asking "What's Different?" is a simple trick to stay awake and avoid operating from old patterns.

The answer to the questions can be anything, regardless if it seems mundane. The human ego wants this answer to be something profound, but actually the simple mechanism of asking the question will access a place of conscious awareness. Even a simple answer—it's sunny today—will help you avoid thinking everything's the same. The more attuned you become to noticing what's different, the more you are strengthening your quantum intelligence.

What worked and what didn't work?

Ask yourself, in the past 24 hours, in your own performance, what worked and what didn't work. You can comment on your own performance only. This is very important. The underlying intention of this part of the check-in is to remove judgment and criticism from your personal field.

Doing this non-judgmental evaluation of your own performance each day is similar to what athletes do in watching game films to see where they can improve their performance. It is merely looking factually at the results without blame, judgment or criticism.

Focus equally on what did work and what didn't work. You will begin to see a pattern in what doesn't work, and you can then develop strategies to change that performance. For example, if your "not work" is that you interrupted someone's conversation, and you see this appearing as a "not work" frequently, you can make the intention to become more aware and stop the behavior.

Another step in this part of the daily check-in is to acknowledge your answers by clapping your hands, applauding yourself. This can seem trivial or silly, however it is very important to celebrate each answer—what worked, what didn't work—equally. Usually in a field of judgment, if you state what didn't work you encounter criticism or blame, from yourself or others. By celebrating your answers, whatever they are, you are acknowledging your recognition of the facts and your intention to be fully aware of your performance.

What is the state of my mind, body and spirit?

Again, the intention of this part of the check-in is for you to live in high noticing and in distinction by seeing the clear separation of your mind, body and spirit. It is common to describe your personal field by referencing only one of these areas. For example, "I woke up with a headache, and my whole day is ruined". When actually doing the check on all areas will show that the headache is in your body, but your mind may be busy and alert, and your spirit may be light and energized. Separating your referencing of these three areas will help you live each day in distinction.

It's important to note that your spirit can only be positive. Spirit is never negative. Words like happy, joyful, expansive, light, soaring, calm, peaceful and creative are words to describe the state of spirit.

What am I grateful for?

Many books have been written on the value of focusing your attention on what's wonderful in your life. Research has shown that people who express gratitude on a frequent basis are more optimistic, feel better about their lives, make more progress towards their goals, and feel higher levels of alertness and energy.

By answering this question each day, you shift your attention to what you do have, rather than what you don't have. That focus allows you to approach your day with more vitality and energy.

What is my intention for today?

What is your intention—one or two sentences that always have an action included. An intention is different from an affirmation. Where an affirmation is a statement—"I am worthy of money"—an intention also involves action. "My intention today is to generate money flow, make six sales calls and have fun doing it."

The power of setting intentions to achieve your vision has been well documented in many books. Manifesting anything you want in your life begins with setting your intention, then taking action towards it.

Holding your own personal energy field is the most critical step in achieving your destiny. The practice of using a daily ritual and performing a daily check-in will result in you being aware, conscious and focused on your vision. And, it will bring in all of the powers of the quantum universe to assist you.

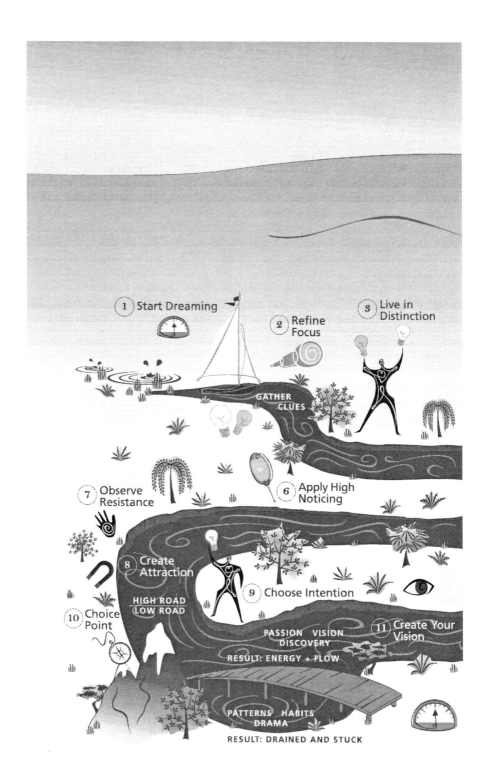

PRINCIPLE 6 APPLY HIGH NOTICING

"Life is a mirror and will reflect back to the thinker what he thinks into it."
—*Ernest Holmes, Founder, Science of Mind*

Journey Notes

> Your physical surroundings are a mirror which reflects the vision you are creating. Use high noticing and pay attention to all of the energetic differences in yourself and your near field.

> What you see in your near field is a reflection of your personal field because your outer world is a reflection of your inner state. If you feel confusion there may still be some form of internal clutter in your life. Likewise, if you feel clear then a feeling of clarity will be reflected back to you.

Creating in Action

Virginia had worked in a division of a large international company for eight years. The years of sitting at a desk and working on a computer had resulted in physical stress: stiffness, joint pain and neck aches. She enjoyed her work but realized that her body was telling her she was ready for a change. It felt like it was time to move on and do something very different.

She became interested in a type of exercise discipline called Pilates. Virginia hired a personal Pilates trainer and started exercising two days a week. Almost instantly she noticed some big differences: the pain and stiffness eased and her body became more comfortable. In addition, she experienced a very pleasant sense of timelessness. She would look at her watch and was surprised to see that hours had gone by. *Her outer world was beginning to reflect her inner state. She practiced high noticing, and paid attention to all of the energetic differences in herself.* She ultimately realized that she wanted to practice Pilates as a full time pursuit. Something that had started as an experiment for her health now provided the clues to a possible new career.

Understanding that her physical surroundings would reflect her vision, Virginia began working at a friend's Pilates studio several days a week on a trial basis. She wondered, "What would that be like if I were to stop working in the corporate world, get certified in Pilates and own my own business? Would I enjoy being an entrepreneur?"

She wanted to experience what it was like to go from being a student to being a teacher, and wondered whether it would "knock her lights out" when it changed from a hobby to a business. By being in action she discovered she was totally lights-on all day. *The change in her outer world reflected the energetic differences of her inner state.* It was much more energizing than she ever thought it might be and thus it exceeded her wildest dreams.

When Virginia got clear about her passion for her new work, the confusion dissipated and she could clearly see her next step, which was to sign up for Pilates instructor training. Realizing that it would take about a year to make the transition, she created a plan so that all of her time, money and energy were focused clearly on her new vision while she still had the financial security of working for a paycheck.

This plan created a bridge that spanned from where she was in present time to where she wanted to be in a year. The bridge plan allowed for time to do the teacher training, become certified, design her studio, purchase needed equipment and line up clients for when she was certified.

In just two years from when she created her vision and got into action, she quit her job, and was in business with a studio fully booked with clients. To this day, both Virginia and her business are thriving as she continues to do what she loves.

Navigational Tools

1. Practice high noticing by paying a lot of attention to what shows up in your personal and near fields.

2. Look at these two fields as if you are looking into a mirror, noticing where there is confusion and where there is clarity. Journal the necessary action steps to remove confusion and create a clear bridge.

3. Use the template of a bridge plan below; fill in some action items.

Here's where you are now.

Here's where you want to go— your lights-on vision.

*Fill in some action items on the bridge
that are energizing
and will move you closer to your vision.*

* Remember that all action steps in present time should be in service to your vision. This avoids busy work.

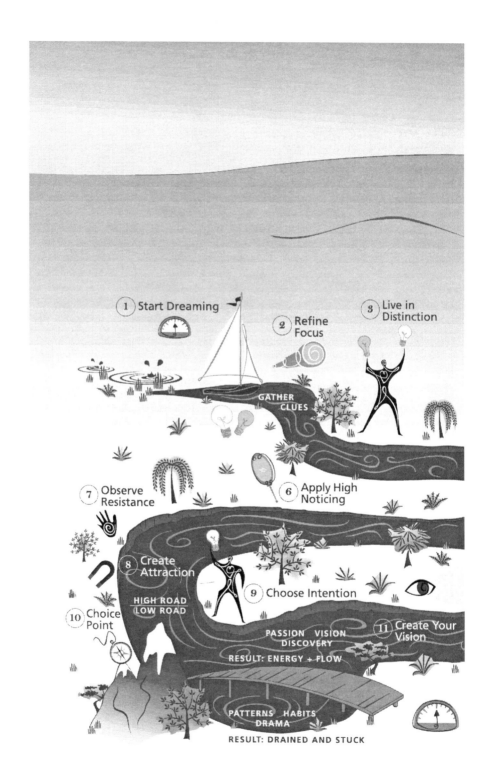

PRINCIPLE 7 OBSERVE RESISTANCE

"The truth will set you free. But, first it will piss you off."—Gloria Steinem, Women's Rights Leader, Publisher

Journey Notes

> What you resist persists. If you go into resistance and create struggle—"I'm going to do this even if it kills me!"—your attention has gone to the resistance instead of your vision, therefore the resistance will continue.

> Resistance and effort are indications that you may have wandered off your path. Negative language ("shoulding" on yourself) is a way to identify a pattern of resistance.

It is a societal norm that effort and struggle are expected in any journey. However, in the Creating journey, effort and struggle are signs of resistance. Although there are times when you must do difficult things to achieve your vision, feeling as though you are hitting your head against a brick wall is a definite clue that you need to shift your attention back to your vision and experience flow.

> Clues that don't show up are signs of resistance. Clues that do show up are signs of flow. As you put your vision into action, pay attention to the clues that don't show up because they are of equal value to the clues that do show up.

Creating in Action

While Susan was in a Master's program in college, she created the idea for a game to be used in schools by teachers and counselors. The purpose of the game was to quickly create connection, foster deeper conversation and ultimately reduce alienation and violence among participants. She was employed as a school counselor and created the game to assist students of all learning styles in developing relationship skills.

The first game board was made out of felt and she cut and sewed everything herself. She played the game in the classroom, where it was very well received; many teachers and counselors requested a copy of the game. It soon became clear that the demand was enough for Susan to create a business producing these games. She was going to be an entrepreneur, owning a production business, in addition to being a full-time counselor. She needed a business plan and money to get started.

Susan entered the Clarity process to get clear about her business vision, including the production needs, and what instructional materials would be necessary to have the game facilitated by others. In terms of production, she wanted to support her local community by using craftspeople in her town. She wanted it to be a "cottage" industry with the game having a hand-crafted look.

Then the resistance started. Many business consultants thought for her to be profitable Susan would need to manufacture the game overseas. She spent months trying to juggle the numbers to make the business plan appeal to the bank. *Her attention was drawn away from the game as she spent countless hours doing paperwork. The problem persisted.* She kept getting her lights knocked out as she ran into negativity from bankers and business advisors. *As she put her vision into action, the clues that didn't show up were of equal value to the clues that did show up.*

In the months of trying to negotiate a bank loan, her business plan became finely tuned. It looked very positive and she was able to get traditional bank loans. However, the business plan also made it clear that she needed to look to other sources for funding. *After months of doing non-creative aspects of number crunching, she shifted her attention back to her vision to create flow.*

The resistance and effort were clues that she may have wandered from her original vision, which was the hand-crafted approach to production and the mission to have the game widely available to teachers and counselors. So with a sound business plan, as well as the support of a professor from her graduate program, she decided to approach private investors to get it launched. When she shifted her attention back to her vision, an angel investor showed up for financial support, and Susan got the monetary flow that she needed.

Susan's business is now fully operational and providing a valuable service to the world. The game is sold in foreign countries, in several languages, and is internet accessible by children all over the world. True to her vision, it is being produced by local people, each of whom Susan personally knows.

She has a relationship with each aspect of producing the game just as it has a relationship with every child who plays it. Her vision to honor community and connections has resulted in the production of a game which mirrors total integrity. The game is a perfect example of the principle: *your outer world is a reflection of your inner state.*

Navigational Tools

1. Be aware of using negative language patterns (but, ought to, should, have to, etc.) and substitute "I choose" statements.
2. Make a list of what didn't show up and what did show up in your vision.
3. Shift your attention to what did show up.

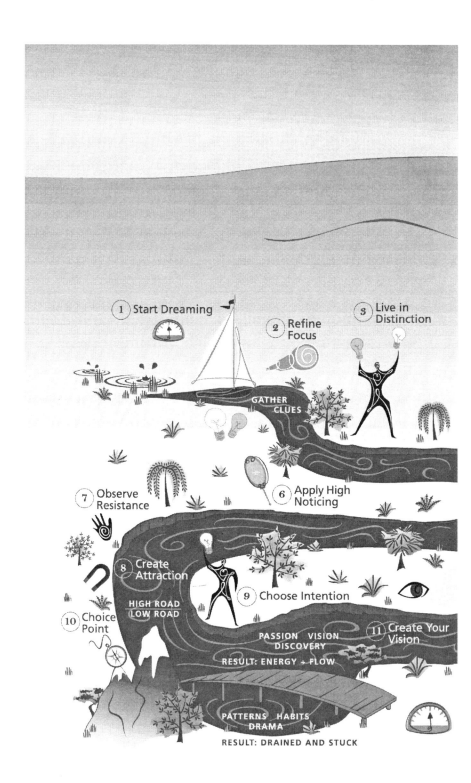

PRINCIPLE 8 CREATE ATTRACTION

"Let yourself be silently drawn by the stronger pull of what you really love."
—*Jalal-Uddin Rumi, 13th century Sufi Poet and Mystic*

Journey Notes

> Energy attracts like energy. Be very clear with your thoughts, words and actions about what you want to attract into your life.

> "If you build it, they will come." The old paradigm was to wait until circumstances were perfect and then act. The new paradigm is to "act as if" in order to create the circumstances. Literally, tell it like you want it to be. This will attract to you what you need to take your vision to the next level.

> Attraction is the opposite magnetic field to resistance. True attraction is effortless and joy-filled.

Creating in Action

When Paula began the Creating the Rest of Your Life™ workshop, she had an executive position in an educational company. She also owned a very beautiful home in a historic district of her city, which she had turned into a bed & breakfast inn.

It was her intention to leave her job as soon as possible in order to focus her attention on her B&B. She envisioned offering more of a retreat experience than just a place to stay for the night. She wanted to attract visitors who desired an opportunity to rest, retreat and learn. However, this intention wasn't clear from the current name of the property. Understanding that *like attracts like,* she decided to use the attraction principle: *"If you build it, they will come."*

When Paula was ready to make the bold move of changing the name of her inn, the universe offered up a synchronous introduction to a historic name that was well known throughout her region. When an article appeared in the local newspaper, Paula discovered the home she owned was deeply connected to the history of her community. She instantly adopted a name that everyone knew reflected that same historical connection.

At the same time, Paula began to advertise her inn as a retreat center. She took one of the rooms and turned it into an area where yoga classes were offered. This created an energetic space for the local community as well as for her guests, who initially had come just for the B&B aspect.

Within a matter of months following these changes, she began to attract her ideal guests, as well as the perfect instructors and staff to support her vision. *Attraction is the opposite magnetic field to resistance.* Soon Paula had visiting holistic speakers on her roster, which enabled her guests to both learn something new and enjoy a very meditative type of exercise during their stay. And, *her attraction was effortless and joy-filled.*

Navigational Tools

1. Use the Energy Meter to make a distinction about the quality of your interactions, relationships and what you are attracting into your vision.

2. Make a distinction between attracting drama (0 = draining) and increasing energy (10 = vitalizing).

3. Notice where your life seems to move forward effortlessly as if you are being pulled along by some unseen current (attraction factor).

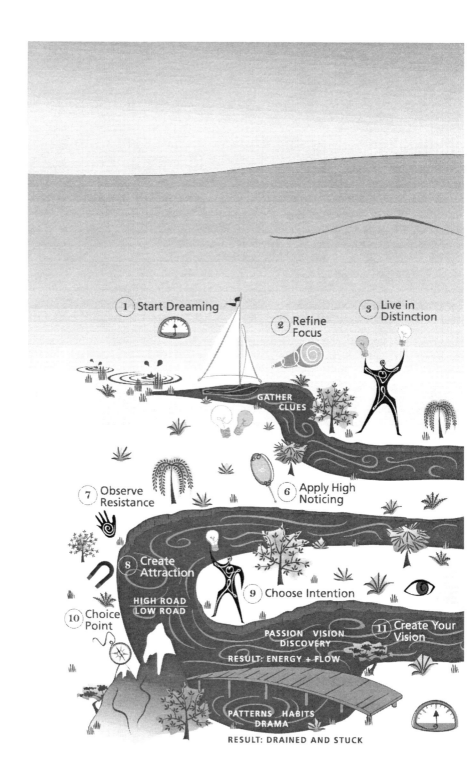

PRINCIPLE 9 CHOOSE INTENTION

"Don't ask yourself what the world needs. Ask yourself what makes you come alive and then go do that. Because what the world needs is people who have come alive."—Harold Thurman, Author, Civil Rights Leader

Journey Notes

> Intention is a strong purpose or vision driven by positive action and direction. Being intentional in thought, word and deed builds a co-creative field where all things are possible. Co-creation is a process that occurs when you release your will and create an opening for guidance.

> You can always tell your intention by the result that is created. Clear intentions = clear results. With clear intention, you will no longer be an "accidental tourist" in your own life.

> Speak and think in terms of what you do want versus what you don't want, using positive terms.

> Be aware of negative speech patterns that can undermine your intentions (should, ought to, but, have to, etc.).

Creating in Action

When Judy began her Clarity work she was co-founder of a well-known, five-member dance company. It was a highly creative group, and they spent many hours rehearsing prior to their performances.

In addition to the physically tiring rehearsals there was the pre-performance stress about details, which proved to be emotionally exhausting. It showed up as an incredible amount of drama around every decision; from the costumes, to the sequence of the performance, to the lighting, to the programs, to just about everything.

Every step along the way contained drama and conflict about creative direction. Even though Judy was doing what she loved to do, and the performance was lights-on for her, going through the last minute drama was definitely taking her lights out. *The thoughts of the individuals involved were creating a reality that was draining.*

Realizing that *intentionality inspires creativity,* she created the intention to model a different, more effective communication style. She called for a team meeting right before rehearsal, when everyone was fresh. Her personal intention was to stay solution-focused and energized; she used a meeting format that focused only on what worked in the performance instead of what didn't work. *Speak and think in terms of what you do want versus what you don't want.*

With her leadership, they all came to the conclusion that the drama was exhausting to everyone and they decided to change the way they were interacting.

Because she made a distinction between drama and energy, and as team leader she brought that to the awareness of the group, their last performance was very different. Everyone went into it energized and excited versus physically tired and drained. *Your thoughts create your reality.*

Judy continues to use these tools in her business and in her personal relationships. She is choosing to stay away from drama and go towards energy. As soon as things get dramatic she takes a time-out and stops. You can always tell your intention by the result that is created.

Navigational Tools

1. Set clear intentions daily by using this template:

   "My intention for today is _____. "

   Negative example: "My intention for today is to not eat junk food."

   This phrasing gives no direction and creates inertia.

   Positive example: "My intention for today is to eat healthfully at all meals."

   This phrasing gives you direction and creates action.

2. Stop, look and listen to your inner voice and choose wisely. Notice

clearly any green lights = go, and red alerts = stop. Follow your energy—not your ideas.

UNDERSTANDING TRANSITION

You've asked for transformation and change. What does that mean in the action phase of real life, where the "rubber meets the road?" Look at the word and you will get a clue. Trans (move) your form (state)...which means that in order to transform, you will have to come undone and then reform in a new way.

Most scholastic education and training did not address these issues, and rarely did you learn enough about it to become comfortable during deep change. In coaching we often say that "Coming Undone 101" and "Living the Mystery 101" wasn't offered in school. You can become scared as change starts to happen, if you aren't well informed.

The following section will be a tutorial to prepare you to journey with ease and grace, and make it more exciting than frightening. It's enjoyable when you know how to navigate! Here's what you need to know.

> *Transition is a natural part of the change process and it creates a zone of being "in between"—no longer where you were and not yet where you are going. This is the transition zone.*
> *Utilizing a vision-led process is synonymous with living in the transition zone.*
> *Visions by their very nature are constantly evolving, adding data (information/intelligence) and shedding data. Visions morph, they "shape shift" naturally.*
> *A key skill for successful journeying is learning how to navigate the transition zone while being relaxed with being "in between", and comfortable with "living the mystery" as you follow your vision.*

> *Transition, transformation, and change are occurring more rapidly than at other times in history.*

Present day circumstances present a big opportunity to create visions for the future differently and more creatively than ever before in history... realizing there is always a "what's next?" leg of your journey that will create lights-on flow and vibrant energy.

Due to the rapidity of change that technology has brought, humans need to acquire new skills to adapt healthfully to continual, moment-to-moment shifts in our environments. You may be afraid of rapid transition based on past experiences that were frightening and painful. That is not unusual! Very few of us got taught how to be in transition. None of us saw "Living the Mystery 101" in our education curricula. As recently as 100 years ago, humans learned to adapt to change by experiencing natural rhythms like flow of seasons, birth and death, waking and sleeping. However, you no longer have that leisure because you live in a world where change is constant rather than minimal.

The truth is you are going to live in a zone of transition more constantly than ever before. Studies are predicting that the 20-something generation is going to have seven full careers over the span of their lifetime, and that the baby boomer generation may live a healthy lifespan of 120 years. If the predictions are accurate, you're going to be around for a long time. You're going to live healthfully with your thought processes and body intact. It's a big call to create visions for the future differently and more creatively.

You are reading this book because you are ready to live your life differently. You have decided to make a change and go on a journey to experience the mystery of your life; explore what is next for you and how the clues that you gather will provide guidance and lead to your destiny. So, fasten your seat belt and enjoy the experience!

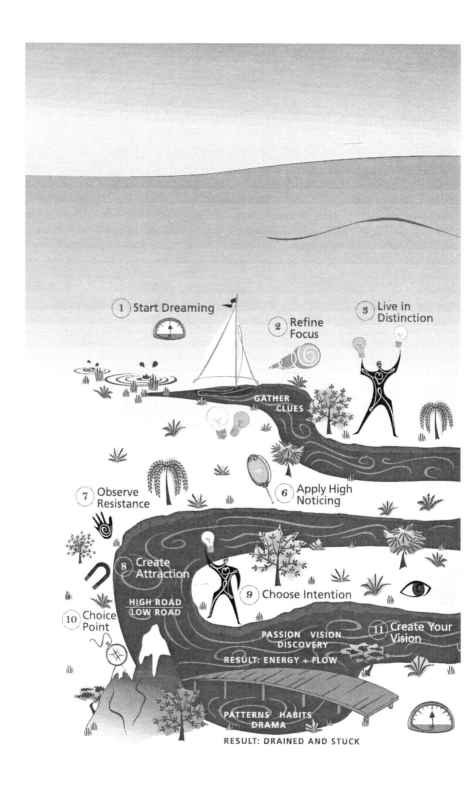

PRINCIPLE 10 MAKE A DECISION— CHOICE POINT

"The Noble Purpose that you awaken to is the divine or God moving in and through you. The movement of Noble Purpose in your life is a prayer, a sacred calling, the "living water" ebbing and flowing through your existence."—Dr. Barry Heermann, Author and Organizational Educator

Journey Notes

Choice Point—Divergent channels appear which create an opportunity to explore different possibilities.

> Every decision you make is a choice point.
> Your choices create your reality.
> Choose Passion over Pattern.

PASSION	TRANSITION ZONE	PATTERN
Above the Line / High Road	**Line / Bridge**	Under the Line / Low Road
Lights-On	**Transformation**	Lights-Off
"The Discovery Channel"	**Challenge**	"The Soap Opera Channel"
Infinite Possibilities	**Paradox**	Limited Possibilities
Solution-focused	**Choice**	Problem-focused
Dharma	**Purpose**	Drama
Energizing	**Mystery**	Draining
Flow	**Shift**	Stagnation
I Am in Charge	**Clarity**	Others Control Me
Curiosity	**Consciousness**	"Been There, Done That"

Transition Zone—The zone of transformation is where the choices that you make transform (change) the results of your actions. In order for change to occur, the form—of objects and people—has to come undone and be formed again, hence the terms transformation and transition.

Creating in Action

Study the Creating Choice Point Guide to verify that you are choosing lights-on and passion when making decisions. Be aware of choosing familiar patterns out of habit.

Navigational Tools

In every moment you are presented with choice points (either above or below the line). They are a universal constant. You are in charge of your choices. The challenge is to remain aware of your options and to always choose *passion over pattern.*

1. To be sure that you are above the line and taking the High Road, ask yourself: "Am I in service to my dreams?"
2. If you think that you are choosing from under the line and taking the Low Road, ask yourself: "Am I in servitude to my patterns?"

GET CLARITY™ CHOICE POINT GUIDE

FOLLOWING
ENERGY FLOW

PASSION
INTENTIONAL

Infinite Possibilities
Clarity
Solution-focused
Observe (mirror)
Dharma (life purpose)
"The Discovery Channel"
Lights-On—Energized

HIGH ROAD

ABOVE THE LINE

CHOICE POINT

CHOICE POINT

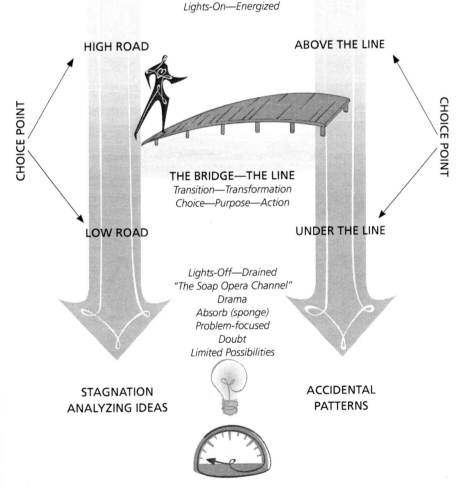

THE BRIDGE—THE LINE
Transition—Transformation
Choice—Purpose—Action

LOW ROAD

UNDER THE LINE

Lights-Off—Drained
"The Soap Opera Channel"
Drama
Absorb (sponge)
Problem-focused
Doubt
Limited Possibilities

STAGNATION
ANALYZING IDEAS

ACCIDENTAL
PATTERNS

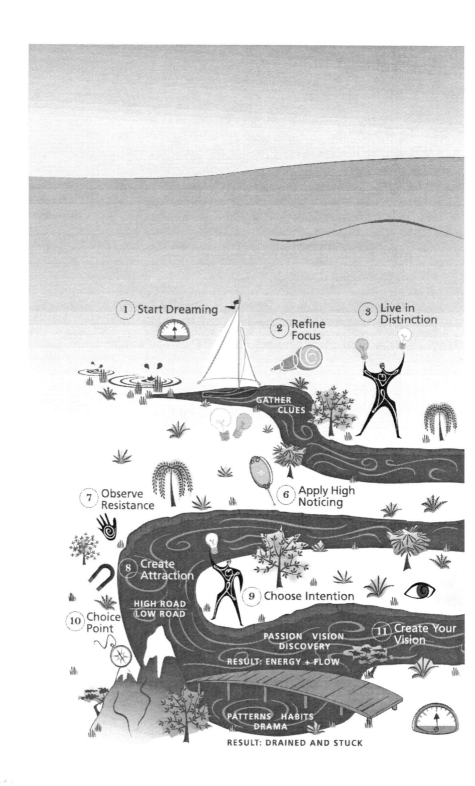

PRINCIPLE 11 CREATE YOUR VISION

"Your vision will become clear only when you can look into your own heart. Who looks outside, dreams; who looks inside, awakes."—Carl G. Jung, Founder of Analytical Psychology

Journey Notes

> Visions must be energetic and lights-on. Visions are the *what* part of your journey. Wherever your attention goes, your energy will follow.

> If you focus on *what* you want (your vision) before going into action, the "how-to's" (the strategies) will clearly present themselves. Culturally, we are taught to focus on strategy before vision. This creates unnecessary pressure and confusion.

Creating in Action

Paul owned a very successful small technology business he had worked in for many years. When he began the Creating the Rest of Your Life™ workshop, he was in his mid-forties and questioning whether he was passionate about owning his company. He enjoyed going to the office and being with the staff. Other than that, he felt that he had completed that phase of his life. There was no excitement or challenge left in it for him. He was not interested in retirement and was very clear that he wanted to stay connected to the business world. His main question was, "what's next that will energize me and keep me passionate?" *He focused on the what part of his journey so that all of his attention would create a lights-on vision.*

During the Clarity process, Paul decided that he would sell the company. His "what's next?" inquiry had presented a new vision, which really lit him up. *Visions must be energetic and lights-on.* He discovered that what he wanted was paradoxical—to both sell the company and remain connected to it.

He stayed focused on what he wanted before he went into any new action. After finding an ideal buyer, he stayed on for a few more years as he developed his vision for a new company. During those years, he made a significant contribution to the integration of his team with the new owners and he kept his own lights on by being involved in the successful transition.

The "how-to's" for his new business venture became very clear. He avoided pressure and confusion as he successfully moved into the strategy phase and launched his new vision.

Navigational Tools

1. At this point, continue to focus on the what, not the how-to. The how-to will be addressed in the next segment of the Creating journey.

2. Make a list of what you want to create in your life, combining all your lights-on clues from the previous principles.

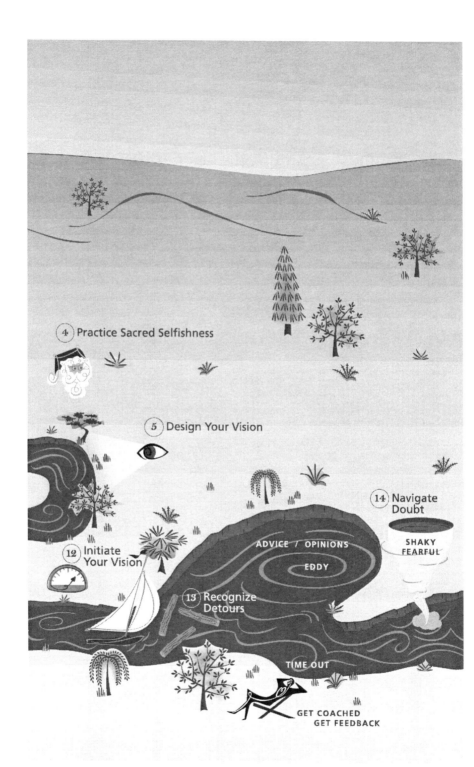

PRINCIPLE 12 INITIATE YOUR VISION

"Vision without action is a daydream. Action without vision is a nightmare."—
Japanese Proverb, Author Unknown

Journey Notes

> Courage is required to initiate your vision. It is a leap of faith.

> Action steps create the movement to reach your vision.

> Flow is the effortless movement towards a vision.

> If you try to go to the how (strategies) before you are very clear about the what (vision) you will deplete your energy, and possibly divert or block the flow of the visioning process.

Creating in Action

When Ellen entered the Creating the Rest of Your Life!™ workshop, she was exhausted and dragging through her days. She felt thoroughly depleted at the end of her usual 70-hour work week. Her career as director of a large non-profit organization was very demanding and she had almost no energy left for her husband and two daughters.

While working downtown, she imagined a place where she could take an hour in the middle of the day, even her lunch hour, and get a relaxing spa treatment to pamper herself as a reward for the really long hours that she put in. But there was no such spa where she could go and, within an hour, receive a range of high quality services. During her visioning session, she got very clear that she wanted to start a downtown day spa where clients, within walking distance of their offices, could receive unique 25-minute "express" spa services.

In order to create movement, Ellen's first action step was to share her vision with her husband, whose support was critical to initiate any change of that magnitude. They would have to risk their financial security and there were multitudes of considerations since neither Ellen nor David had been entrepreneurs before. They had always been employees and were used to job security and benefits. They were in their late 40's and could anticipate early retirement in 10 years. *Courage was required to initiate her vision. This began to look like a leap of faith.*

Ellen wasn't sure if she could survive until retirement at the rate she was working; she felt that she was missing out on important events in her daughters' lives. It was imperative that she find a way to make her dream come true without risking their life savings. *She needed to do some in-depth research to create movement, and bring David some facts, which she did.*

In fact, she took about a year doing this preparatory homework—gathering information about costs to initiate a day spa, the time it would take to be profitable, and the demographics for an ideal location. She enjoyed the research process and would often look at her watch to realize that hours had gone by when it felt like only minutes had passed. This was very energizing and different from the fatigue that she felt at other times. *The flow she experienced was the effortless movement towards her vision.*

The next step was a visioning session where Ellen and David balanced two key facts, which emerged from the research. First, creating a spa was a very costly venture and second, her vision was at the forefront of an emerging business trend and predicted to be worthy of investment. *By using the researched numbers as a guide for action, Ellen went into initiating her vision while realizing that, given their lack of entrepreneurial expertise, this was a total leap of faith.*

Although they had fears to face and overcome, Ellen and David were confident that she could initiate her vision and have a successful outcome for herself and the whole family. In that leap of faith, she was well supported as she got out into action.

If Ellen had tried to go to the how (strategy) and gotten buried in the myriad of details before she was crystal clear about the what (vision), she would have depleted her energy even further. And, she could have actually diverted or blocked the initiating process altogether.

Navigational Tools

1. Create a vision map (collage or simple drawings) to illustrate your vision. Hang it in a visible place as a constant reminder of where you want to go.

2. Fill in the how-to section below, correlating the strategies closely to your vision.

VISION (What)	STRATEGY (How-to)

3. Create an action plan by prioritizing the strategies.

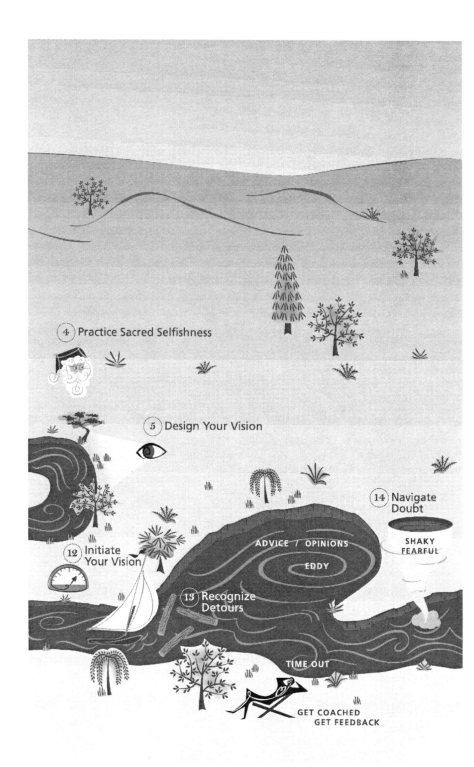

PRINCIPLE 13 RECOGNIZE DETOURS

"One day you finally knew what you had to do, and began, though the voices around you kept shouting their bad advice...but little by little as you left their voice behind, the stars began to burn through the sheets of clouds, and there was a new voice which you slowly recognized as your own, as you strode deeper and deeper into the world, determined to do the only thing you could do."—Mary Oliver, Author and Poet

Journey Notes

Detour—A divergence from the intended route, usually caused by well-meaning advice or opinion rather than feedback .

> Advice and opinion are inherent in an analytic operating system.
> Advice is heady and idea-based. It sounds like: "good idea, bad idea, you should, if I were you..."
> Feedback is a natural part of an energetic operating system.
> Feedback mirrors your enthusiasm. It sounds like: "that lights you up, tell me more about..."

Once you have initiated your vision and gone into flow, detours are to be expected. They are routine and part of every journey. On the Creating Journey Map it looks like encountering a log jam. This usually happens when you start to share your dream and someone gives you well-intentioned advice or opinion, and begins to tell you what you "should" be doing. As you listen, you may notice that you feel drained or irritable. In other words, they have "knocked your lights out." This is an example of "friendly" advice; it is different than "factual advice" from an expert.

The way to get back into action and return to your vision is to find someone to give you positive feedback. Finding that person means that you will go to someone who is willing to suspend their judgment, opinions and advice, and they should simply tell you what energizes you. Accurate feedback is not about the other person and their "great" ideas for you. It will sound like this: "I don't really understand it myself but it really lights you up."

At this point, you've found a support person who is willing to use an energetic operating system as opposed to an analytic operating system. This person becomes your strategic ally. It is important to have at least one unbiased person like this on your team.

Having a strategic ally will make it easier to stay true to your vision and avoid the pitfall of "paralysis by analysis."

Creating in Action

David and Ellen's story continues with their experiences as they launched their first venture into the spa world.

Remember they started with an "express spa" business model, knowing they had much to learn and many systems to develop. However, their bigger vision included a large "destination spa," which could provide a broad range of services and classes.

During the year that they spent gathering facts and information for their first spa, they found a piece of riverfront property that would be a beautiful site for their future destination spa. They got excited about the possibility of this riverfront location. It was within driving distance of a developing affluent suburb and they envisioned the beauty that was possible if they built a spa there exactly as they imagined it.

They gathered information, including preliminary architectural plans and actual building costs. *Advice and opinion are inherent in an analytic operating system.* The numbers that they got were discouraging. It was too costly and would not be profitable for a first venture. This disappointing factual advice was accurate and, when they looked at the numbers, they got their "lights knocked out." Ellen and David became unclear and started swirling around about the choices. *They became scattered by going to the biggest and most far away vision rather than staying focused on the next lights-on vision step.*

Instead of giving up her dream, Ellen hired a Clarity-trained coach for feedback. *Feedback is a natural part of an energetic operating system.* She revisited her vision and made sure that she was in flow toward her lights. The coaching reminded her that her core vision was to launch a downtown express spa that would be of service to working people in the neighborhood. She was lights-on about locating it in an existing historical building.

Ultimately, she and David rented a property in an old building and renovated it. Fortunately, the landlord assisted with part of the cost of the renovation because it also upgraded his property. *They eliminated scatter, regained their focus and got back into action when they were coached with positive feedback.* They were able to get back into their dream, using incremental steps that were affordable and made sense both analytically and energetically.

The coaching feedback reminded them that it wasn't part of their launch vision to own land and build from the ground up. Having a strategic ally made it easier to stay true to their vision and avoid the pitfall of "paralysis by analysis."

Navigational Tools
1. Return to your vision. Re-focus and direct your energy by studying your vision map.
2. Take a time-out. Find a person who is willing to act as a mirror to your vision. Ask them to coach you by giving accurate feedback based on your lights as you state your vision to them.
3. Take note of the feedback that you have been given.
4. Remember: when you are faced with "friendly" advice, don't take anything personally. Although well-meaning, other people often use their own fear and worry to "protect" you, which keeps you from initiating your vision.

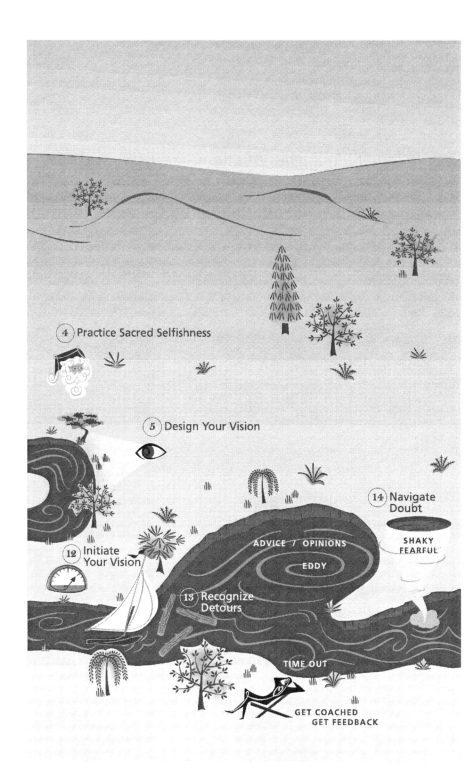

PRINCIPLE 14 NAVIGATE DOUBT

"Don't be afraid your life will end; be afraid that it will never begin."—Grace Hansen, Author and Poet

Journey Notes

Doubt—An undecided state of mind creating uncertainty and inertia. Doubt is a normal part of any journey to passion.

> Doubt your doubt, not your dream. Everyone encounters doubt on their path. When doubt enters, you become shaky, fearful and uncertain. It creates inertia from the uncertainty of what choice to make or what action to take. The voice of doubt asks repetitive questions which will not elicit any useful information, such as "What was I thinking?!" It becomes very circular and produces no useful answers or intelligent facts.

> Face your fears of the unknown. Reduce fear by shifting your attention to gathering facts. Fear predominates when you don't have enough information to make an intelligent choice.

Creating in Action

When Jackie entered the Creating coaching process, she was ready to embark on a huge career change. With more than 20 years experience in personal and corporate organizing, she was ready to launch her own business as a professional organizer. She was excited about becoming an entrepreneur and the freedom it would provide. She was more than ready to create her own hours and be in charge of the projects she worked on. But she was equally fearful about living without a paycheck and using her savings until her business took off.

Jackie decided to face her fears of the unknown and get into action as an entrepreneur. Realizing the unknowns that scared her most were the fluctuations and uncertainty of income, she gathered information about income potential from other people in her field.

She got a clear picture of when to expect the finances to flow and then was able to turn her attention to generating leads to find clients. Jackie found that she loved public speaking about clearing clutter, finding balance, simplifying, and how that process transformed people's lives. She decided that she wanted to write a book offering a simple system to make life easier for people who were inundated with paper clutter.

That is when doubt entered. Jackie had never written a book before and she doubted her ability to write one. So, she joined writers' associations and started to get information from people who had similar experiences. Even though her clients were asking for a book from her, and she had gathered a lot of supportive information, *she remained fearful and uncertain. Inertia set in, she got stuck and didn't proceed for almost a year.*

Finally, with some coaching to doubt her doubt instead of her dream, she began writing. The book was published within a year; her business flourished and has provided her with much happiness for many years.

Jackie now helps other writers to organize their book writing process. "Doubting the doubt" ultimately created an additional revenue source for her expertise.

Navigational Tools

1. To get out of doubt and fear of the unknown, shift your attention by gathering information.

2. Ask seven questions related to your vision. This will give you enough knowledge and intelligent answers to continue with certainty. For example, if you are considering relocating you might: consult the internet; talk to a realtor; look at a map; talk to other people who live there; contact the Chamber of Commerce; and investigate community services and employment opportunities.

Armed with this information your doubt and fear will be greatly reduced. Write your questions and answers below.

COMPASS POINT 3—SEEING ENERGY IN PATTERNS

Energy in the human body usually shows up as a cluster that is recogniz-able as a pattern. These patterns are discernible in your personal field and the fields of others around you. While you are traveling on the Creating journey, an awareness of them will make it easier to navigate. Like celestial navigation where seeing star patterns in the night sky guides your physical journey, accurate pattern recognition in your personal field will guide your Creating journey.

Since energy is an invisible force it is easier to see the effects of it in clusters or patterns. This requires high noticing because you can't actually see energy. You can only see and feel the results of energy in your body when you are vitalized or drained.

There are multitudes of energy patterns, however, there are four that we think are the most useful for you to be acquainted with for the purposes of the Creating journey. Those four patterns are; light and shadow, monkey mind, archetypes, and chakras.

In general, energy patterns share these qualities:

> They are neutral, neither negative nor positive.

> They contain information which is valuable to your movement.

> They are invisible forces and can only be seen by observing the effects and results of their actions.

Examples: Wind—movement of air produces results ranging from leaves rustling to storms. Electricity—movement of current produces results ranging from on/off appliances to power grids. Human energy (chi)—flow throughout the body produces results ranging from drained (lights-off) to energized (lights-on).

> Energy patterns generally operate subconsciously. It is critical that you bring these patterns into your conscious awareness in order for you to create flow in your life.

> Flow is produced as a result of becoming conscious of (discovering) the draining energy patterns, and intentionally using strategies to return to actions and thoughts that energize you (recovery). This becoming conscious and using intentional strategies to change your thoughts and actions is called **Rapid Discovery, Rapid Recovery.**

The Energy Pattern of Light and Shadow

Light patterns are defined as what energizes you, and gets you into flow. Shadow patterns are defined as what will stop you, by creating inertia. Using a movie metaphor, it is like recognizing your Luke Skywalker tendencies and your Darth Vader tendencies, the light and dark side characters from Star Wars.

Lack of knowledge of your shadow pattern (dark side) is a major factor to stopping you from realizing your full potential. The more clarity you have about your light and shadow patterns, the easier it will be to recognize your shadow patterns.

The shadow is always present. However, if you keep your attention on the light, it will lose its power. The key is to focus on the light; on what energizes you every day.

Examples of shadow patterns include: fear, obligation, self-pity, doubt, anxiety, quitting, competition, imitation, compromise, guilt, pressure, martyrdom, attachment, envy, apathy, greed, passing judgment, overdoing, control, self-importance, lust, and perfectionism.

Success in navigating the Creating Journey Map will be enhanced when you acquire this knowledge. Most of you are familiar with aspects of what lights you up, however few of you are familiar with your shadow behavior. It can seem scary and challenging to learn about it. However, what is really scary is not knowing your shadow. It's like "an accident waiting to happen." Not knowing the behavior pattern that will stop you is like being in a fog. Your shadow will appear and blind-side you just when you are gaining clarity and momentum. To paraphrase a famous line from an early radio show, "Only the shadow knows." If "only the shadow knows," you will not live the life of your dreams.

All people who successfully manifest their visions recognize—rapid discovery —and move past their shadow behavior by having a willingness to switch focus back to lights-on energy—rapid recovery. They then go into action by doing any action that lights them up. This is a simple truth—if you follow your light you will get more light, more energy. When you do something that is energizing, you will get more energy. It's that simple.

Remember that the shadow is always there—it never goes away. The empowerment strategy is to be truthful about when you are in your shadow, and quickly shift your attention to your journey.

Become easy with your shadow, know that what you focus on expands, and turn your focus back to your destiny. In all seriousness and lightness at the same time, have fun looking at the list of shadow possibilities below, and find one that is your primary "Achilles' heel."

Actions to Discover Your Shadow Pattern

1. Look at the example of shadows below and pick one that you think could be your primary shadow. Note that you can pick a "second runner-up" if you are undecided, but that is all. Certainly you have experienced many of these patterns. However, there is one primary shadow that will take you out of your game and stop you from reaching your vision. Concentrate on finding the *one* which could sabotage your destiny. Be honest!

Examples of Shadow Patterns

> Fear, obligation, self-pity, doubt, anxiety, quitting, competition, limitation, compromise, guilt, pressure, martyrdom, attachment, envy, apathy, greed, passing judgment, overdoing, control, self-importance, lust, and perfectionism.

2. Create a character that can represent a spoof of the shadow that you picked. The character should bring humor when you think of it. It is important to make light with your shadow.

The Energy Pattern of Monkey Mind

Monkey mind—a Buddhist expression which states that when you try to be calm, the mind jumps around like a "drunken monkey"—describes the self-critical or danger chatter (heard as an inner voice) of the human mind. Monkey mind has its physiological origins in the "fight or flight" syndrome. Immediately when threat is perceived, the hypothalamus secretions stimulate the pituitary to secrete a message to the adrenal glands, and they release cortisol thus elevating blood sugar for extra energy to act. This cascade of glandular events prepares your body to be ready for action when it senses a potential threat. Its purpose is to warn you of danger.

Change is interpreted as threatening and dangerous to this primitive alert system which was formed in your body when change was a relatively rare occurrence.

The constant change of today's world sends a "change = danger" signal, and cortisol is produced. Therefore, your body is on adrenalin alert almost constantly (often at night) in response to perceived threat of danger.

This adrenalin alert can show up as an energy pattern of doubt, worry, anxiety, disturbed sleep, restlessness, fatigue, alienation, hopelessness, and inability to focus.

The most noticeable result of the monkey mind chatter is how it keeps you distracted from being in present time. Here's an example of how it works. Suppose you are at lunch with a friend, engaged in a lights-on conversation. Your body is sitting there, your brain mind is engaged and conversing, and all of a sudden your monkey mind starts chattering in the background about trivial matters. Your body is sitting there but you're not fully present. It looks like you're there and sometimes you can even be in an actual conversation but meanwhile monkey mind is running a whole other conversation about something that you haven't gotten done, or there's never enough time, or what you should be doing, and so on. It is a constant din going on in the background. It is usually judging and criticizing you. This is going on the whole time you are at lunch and even though it looks like you're there and your body is in place, your attention is somewhere else. You are scattered and distracted. This is literally an internal monologue taking charge of a situation.

After many hours of coaching conversations with clients, Cathy has observed some common patterns of monkey mind conversations everyone experiences. While not a scientific study, her observations are useful and add humor to a deeper understanding of this energy pattern. A few of her observations are:

> Monkey mind speaks constantly and is rarely quiet.
> Monkey mind has the speech sophistication and sentence structure of a five year old child.
> The monkey mind speech pattern is repetitive, like a monologue, repeating similar sentences over and over again, almost like a tape running constantly in your head.
> The monkey mind speech contents are negative and laden with worst-case scenarios.

Imagine that if you pay attention to monkey mind, it is like having a worried five year old in charge of your life.

Since many people are aware of this constant din, there are a number of meditative practices aimed at quieting the mind. It is difficult to turn it off and quiet the mind. Dedicated practitioners say that even after years of meditating for long periods at a time, they consider it "a win" if they achieve quiet for a few minutes at a sitting. Knowing that monkey mind is running the show, and knowing that the astute masters are only able to turn it off for minutes at a time, then how do you as an ordinary mortal live your life consciously and override the tapes in your head?

Fortunately, there is a way. It emerged as a pattern that Cathy was able to recognize through the years of coaching people to make their dreams come into reality. Whenever clients got stuck by monkey mind, Cathy coached them to recognize and acknowledge the chatter while continuing to stay in action toward their dream. Instead of resisting it by focusing on meditating longer in an attempt to push monkey mind away, they accepted and acknowledged its presence.

Accepting the presence of monkey mind while simultaneously staying focused on what lights you up works and has proven to be very successful. It is a great exercise in letting go, and this strategy of releasing resistance and going into acceptance creates a powerful shift. That is how ordinary people have successfully stayed on their path while monkey mind chatters to them.

Just understanding that there is a physiological reason for its presence is also helpful. Monkey mind is a necessary safety scan which gives you important clues about whether to approach or avoid a given situation. Remember that what started as a "fight or flight" alert in the primitive, limbic brain has enlarged into a constant "change = danger" message. This is not surprising because you are not in the relative quiet of the caveman days anymore. While very effective at warning you about passing threats that require immediate action, your stress responses are less effective against constant, low-level annoyances like hectic daily traffic. You are now in a culture that is in constant change with bells ringing, alarms going off, sirens wailing, cars zooming by, and people and crowds pushing on you. The limbic brain, wired thousands of years ago, perceives this as threatening and dangerous. Consequently, it's on duty a lot, even disturbing your sleep at times, literally working constantly. This stress can have negative effects on your health when it is chronic instead of occasional.

However, it is important to remember that this primitive "red alert" system is very necessary to your survival. It is precisely this early alert system that is working every time you approach an unfamiliar person or setting. Do you want to walk into a poorly lit parking garage late at night and not have your "red alert" system functioning? Absolutely not! That's its job—to scan an environment, assess if there is danger present, and cue you whether to approach or avoid. Don't fire the system—it is essential to your safety and is always welcome for the rare time when you may actually be in danger.

Again the key to successfully navigating the Creating Journey is that of pattern recognition—*rapid discovery* and then *rapid recovery*. When you get a shaky and doubtful feeling, the primary recovery strategy is to be conscious of the monkey mind monologue, without resisting it or agreeing with it. If you are in an unfamiliar environment, use a "stop-look-listen" scan and ask, "Am I in danger?" "Is there anything here that I am getting alerted to?" Thankfully, most of the time the answer is no, and your safety is assured. This mind-body connection is very powerful.

Another recovery strategy involves finding a relaxation practice which appeals enough to you that you will practice it regularly. The mind–body connection has been studied in depth for several decades and the relationship between emotion and health has created many practices that work. A recent Newsweek Health for Life report stated that nearly half of all Americans engaged in mind-body practices which ranged from yoga to deep breathing to meditation to hypnosis to guided imagery to labyrinth walking. The same report stated that nearly one out of two Americans said that they prayed—perhaps the oldest and most basic form of mind-body medicine.

Actions to Discover Your Monkey Mind Monologue

Find a mind–body practice for relaxation, and apply these three universal principles as a process to stay focused on your vision. It is a very effective way to get out of this conundrum with your monkey mind. They are:

1. What you resist persists, so acknowledge the monologue by scanning your environment to assure safety which initiates *rapid discovery.*

2. What you focus on expands, so never empower monkey mind by agreeing with it. Quickly turn your attention to your lights and that will shift your focus.

3. Where you put your attention is where your energy goes. Keep your attention focused on your lights-on plan and go into action with at least one energizing step which creates *rapid recovery.*

The Energy Pattern of Archetypes

Archetypes are patterns of consciousness that are recognizable collectively and individually, like familiar characters. Archetypes are impersonal patterns of influence that are both ancient and universal and they become personalized when you recognize them as playing a part in your journey.

Archetypal patterns can give you clues to your own destiny because they contain lessons for you to learn about the strengths and weaknesses of each pattern. Your challenge is to face and recognize the opportunity to learn the inherent lesson by acknowledging it, overcoming the shadow it represents and developing your personal power.

The expression of an archetype is unique to you and these expressions interact with the archetypes of other people in your life.

The subject of archetypes is a complete study in itself, so we will briefly address archetypes here in this chapter and suggest that you study them more if they interest you. At the end of this section is information to guide your future studies. We include them as patterns because they are such an important part of everyday life. It is almost impossible not to be aware of them. You talk about them in everyday conversations when you describe people. Characters in books, movies, theatre, and television are based on archetypes.

A simple way to define an archetype is that they are characters with light and shadow persona, some of which you identify with and many that you don't. You can recognize the presence of an archetype when you comment that someone acts as if they are a queen, or a warrior, or a rebel, or a savior and so on. Although it is easiest to see in someone else, with some practice you will know your personal archetypes and the guidance they offer. The usefulness to you on the Creating journey is to be aware of what they are, and then make a choice, using free will, to determine the lesson that you wish to learn.

Each archetype has a light lesson and a shadow lesson. For example, the queen archetype: on the light side would the benevolent queen who watches over her domain generously for the good of all; on the shadow side would be the wicked queen who only looks out for herself, or a drama queen who always demands attention and creates crises to draw attention to herself.

Another example is the boss archetype we are all familiar with. On the light side would be the leader who empowers the team through trust and delegation. On the shadow side would be the dictator who weakens the team through distrust and micro-management. Another example is the figurehead boss who only shows up for appearance sake and is non-supportive to the team. As with the queen, there are many more ways to act out the boss archetype.

Again the key to successfully navigating the Creating journey is that of pattern recognition, *rapid discovery* and then *rapid recovery* in pursuit of your vision.

Because there are hundreds of archetypes to learn about, we recommend that you use Carolyn Myss as a teacher. She is an excellent source on this subject and has made it easy and fun to discover your archetypes through her books and seminars. Her book, *Sacred Contracts: Awakening Your Divine Potential*, provides a fascinating and exciting exploration into this subject. To view her seminar schedule, see her website www.myss.com.

Actions to Discover Your Archetypes

1. Make note of the archetypal pattern or patterns that may be operative for you by listing the characters that you know have been used to describe you, by yourself or others.
2. Ask what is the lesson or message it presents to you, and write that down.

The Energy Pattern of the Chakra System

Chakras are energy centers located in the body that are aligned with the spinal column from the base of the spine to the crown of the head. They act as conduits through which universal energy and information flows.

There are seven chakras located in the body and these centers are storehouses and transmitters for energy.

LOCATION	RELATES TO
Chakra 1—the base of the spine	Grounded Action
Chakra 2—the genital area	Creativity
Chakra 3—the solar plexus	Personal Power
Chakra 4—the heart	Love and Passion
Chakra 5—the throat	Expression
Chakra 6—the forehead	Vision
Chakra 7—the crown of the head	Inspired Thoughts

The chakras receive, store and transmit energy and information by interacting with the electromagnetic energy field surrounding you and transforming it into the energy that sustains your life.

When chakras are open and aligned, energy travels freely, easily, and abundantly throughout the body. It is important for your total health and well being that the energy freely flows back and forth between you and the universe, without blockages.

The chakra system originated among healers and seers in ancient India. Thousands of years old, it is respected and used today by many Western doctors and inter-disciplinary healers. The chakra system is mentioned in this book because it is a way of relating to energy and energy patterns. Having a chakra system perspective will enhance your awareness of how energy flows within your body (your personal field) and how that energy flow is in a constant and dynamic exchange with universal energy (your near field and the remote field).

Powerful creative energy flows freely when the seven chakra conduit, much like a column, is aligned and open. You may have heard the term Kundalini which refers to energy stored in the 1st or "root" chakra, often represented as a snake, which when released opens and aligns the whole chakra system with a stimulation of powerful creative energy. When that powerful energy is aligned with "the path of the heart" at the 4th chakra, it flows to the mind and makes the "heart mind" connection. It feels like the rush or surge of energy when you have an "Aha" experience of being suddenly clear, and it is closely related to the physiology of lights-on.

In the Creating journey, the 4th chakra, the heart center, is the key piece of information for discovering what you love doing. You can't get true clarity through your head alone. You can't think your way to desire. "You must follow your heart" has often been said in colloquialisms, and now there is strong scientific data that supports that wisdom, thanks to the work of the Institute of HeartMath. Visit the website www.heartmath.com for more data.

The "heart mind" connection makes sense scientifically because the magnetic field of the heart is approximately a thousand times stronger than that of the brain. According to data from the Institute of HeartMath, the heart has enough power that your electrocardiogram can be measured in every cell of your body, from head to toe.

When you feel upset, there is such a body-wide sense of disharmony that the effects can show up on an electrocardiogram. Likewise, when you are calm and peaceful, the waves on the electrocardiogram are smoother and more coherent. Interesting magnetometer data from the Institute of Heart Math shows the heart signal does not stop at the skin, but radiates into the space around you, and the field of the heart can actually be measured four to five feet away. This data relates closely to teachings of the chakra system by showing the scientific evidence that when you connect to your heart, you are transmitting energy from your personal field and receiving feedback from the near field, and back and forth. These back and forth interactions are important to notice because heart connected actions and living lights-on are the same thing.

You don't need an in-depth knowledge of the chakra system to get an idea of how the alignment of energy centers works. Viewing the diagram on the right will give you an image that is easy to understand. We call it an alignment model for flow when: your ideas (7) connect to your heart (4) and direct your actions (1).

This is an energetic representation of "walking (1) your (4) talk (7). " This alignment is what we often refer to in Clarity coaching as integrated and authentic action, and it is lights-on.

ENERGY FLOW PATTERN OF THE CHAKRA SYSTEM

YOUR PERSONAL FIELD

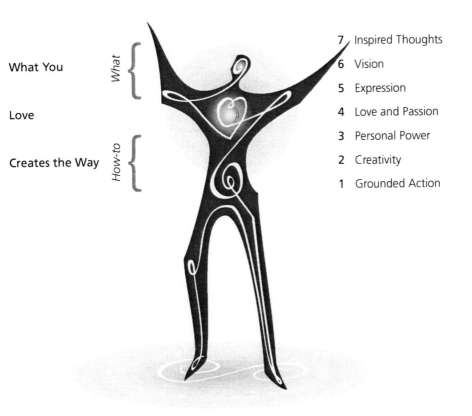

7 Inspired Thoughts

6 Vision

5 Expression

4 Love and Passion

3 Personal Power

2 Creativity

1 Grounded Action

What You

What

Love

Creates the Way

How-to

ALIGNMENT MODEL OF FLOW

7 - 4 - 1
Creates Balance and Manifestation

Your ideas (7) connect to your heart (4) and direct your actions = (1)
You Walk Your Talk

PRINCIPLE 15 UNDERSTAND MONKEY MIND

"All we are is the result of what we have thought."—Buddha, Founder of Buddhist Religion

Journey Notes

Monkey Mind—A concept rooted in Buddhist teachings. It describes a self-critical aspect of the human mind, which provides a constant, ongoing commentary of judgment and criticism, filled with worst case scenarios.

> Monkey mind diverts your attention from present time by swinging your thoughts between doubt and worry.

> Doubt makes up dramatic stories about negative experiences from the past; it is fictional history tripping.

> Worry makes up scary stories and worst case scenarios about the future; it is fictional future tripping.

> Neither doubt nor worry will give you accurate information upon which you can base your future decisions.

Creating in Action

Matt is a very talented musician. After graduating from college he indulged his love of music by playing guitar with local artists, both on stage and in the studio. He was highly regarded in the local music community and developed a reputation as the guitarist for artists to use for high quality studio recording.

When a well-known entertainment company announced a local guitar audition for a new show opening in Los Angeles, Matt and several hundred other guitarists auditioned. As luck and talent would have it, he was one of the very few who got called back for further screening the next day.

On the one hand, he was very excited about the possibility of being part of the show with all of the benefits, both creative and financial. On the other hand, it would mean a big change in his life for both him and his fiancée, Ann. They would be required to move to Los Angeles. Ann would have to close her very successful consulting business and re-establish herself with a new clientele. There was a lot to be considered if he were chosen.

That was when Matt's monkey mind, sensing a big change coming, became very active. It absolutely went into overdrive. His world was now open to change and transition, which is interpreted as danger. His system went on adrenaline alert almost immediately; he couldn't tell if he was excited, scared, or both.

That night, instead of resting, his monkey mind kept him up all night saying things like: "you're no good, you'll never make it, and you don't deserve a big break like this." *Monkey mind diverted his attention from the huge opportunity presented to him by swinging his thoughts between doubt and worry.* By the next morning, Matt had convinced himself that he wasn't going to go to the audition because he just wasn't good enough to be chosen. He had thought it over and he felt it just wasn't a good fit for him.

Overnight, monkey mind had not only convinced Matt that he was no good and really wouldn't make it, but it had also convinced him that he didn't even want the position. *Doubt makes up dramatic stories about negative experiences from the past; it is fictional history tripping.*

Luckily, he mentioned his decision to Ann, who called immediately for some Clarity coaching. Cathy coached Matt to go and do the audition because he had nothing to lose and everything to gain. He literally made it to the audition at the last minute and was chosen and hired for the new show. He was totally lights-on at the outcome, and very amazed that monkey mind and negative self talk had come within minutes of taking him out of his game. *Neither doubt nor worry will give you accurate information upon which you can base your future decisions.*

Matt and Ann faced the challenge of relocating her business; they successfully transitioned to a new city where they knew no one. It has been an excellent move for both of them. As for Matt, he loves the show; loves the position; is financially set and stable; and has had free time to work on other creative projects. He went from monkey mind almost stopping him, to overcoming fictional obstacles, to realizing his dream and living it.

Navigational Tools

1. What are the doubt and fear saying? Write down the predominant thoughts.

2. Now that the statements are out of your head and on paper, read them and decide if they are real or imagined. To assist you in this process, refer to the following clues about the monkey mind monologue:

> Perceives *any change* as danger.
> Constantly talking.
> Repetitive monologue.
> Speech sophistication of a five year old child.

As you look at your statements objectively, you will discover they are imagined or fictional and they will lose their power over you.

PRINCIPLE 16 RETURN TO YOUR VISION

"A dream collage is pictures of your goals. It is like your future photo album."—
Bo Bennett, Author and Motivational Speaker

Journey Notes

> Dreams that are passionate and connected to your heart take on a life of their own.

> Visions have to stay visible to remain vital.

Creating in Action

After eight years as a successful entrepreneur, having conquered all of her fears, doubts and monkey mind, Jackie decided it was time for a new vision.

She returned to her original vision and took a look at what she had accomplished in her eight years as a solo entrepreneur. She knew she loved being an organizational coach, guiding and transforming her clients' lives as they cleared their clutter and made room for new beginnings. That was a major lights-on for her.

However, working alone was becoming lights-off. During a Clarity coaching session she realized that she once again wanted to be part of a team and work for someone else. Jackie was relieved to realize that she was tired of doing everything by herself. She was ready for a new vision and the major changes that would result.

Initially, she struggled with the thought of giving up her business. Monkey mind was saying that she had failed as an entrepreneur, despite all objective results to the contrary. After wrestling with her monkey mind and making the decision to "doubt her doubts," she set out to find her perfect team. *Knowing that visions have to stay visible to remain vital, Jackie created another vision map.* Guided by that vision, she wrote the perfect job description from the perspective of what she was passionate about and loved to do.

Jackie then shifted her attention onto searching for the perfect group that would be a fit for her. She focused on the search, trusting all of the knowledge and experience that she had gained from working on her own.

In order to make time, she started to cut back on her number of organizing clients and started to refer them to colleagues. This was very scary, as her income was temporarily reduced while she devoted time to the search. She created an intention to make her sphere of influence bigger by affiliating with "the perfect people for the perfect pay," and started the process of submitting her resume to select organizations.

After several weeks, she was contacted by a design and remodeling firm that wanted to add a professional organizer to their staff. It presented a wonderful opportunity to do many things that she had dreamed of doing with a team to help things happen.

Jackie accepted the position and in doing so has taken her business to the next level, as well as theirs. It is a major "win–win" for both parties. *Her dream was passionate and connected to her heart, and it took on a life of its own.*

Navigational Tools

1. Shift your attention away from any negative thoughts from your monkey mind; create a new lights-on vision map.
2. Place this map in a place where you can easily see it, using it as visual guide as you go forward.
3. Use the space below to create a new list of action steps to bring the vision into action.

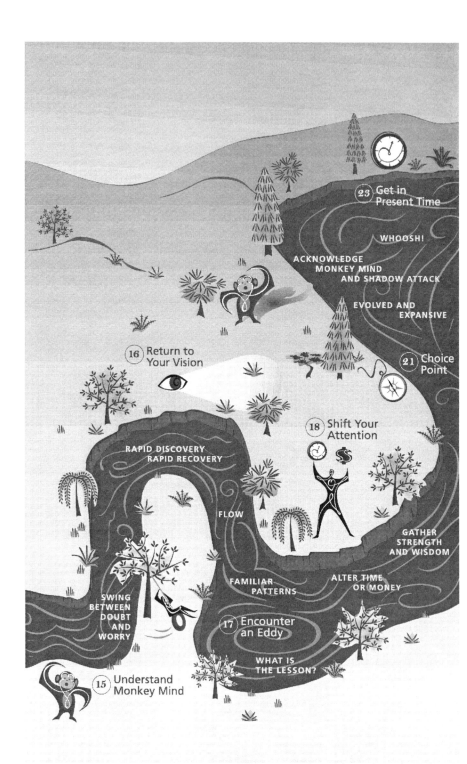

PRINCIPLE 17 ENCOUNTER AN EDDY

"I've taken lessons all my life just because I wanted to, but it seemed a waste not to take advantage of what I've learned."—Tony Williams, Jazz and Rock Musician

Journey Notes

Eddy—A circular movement of water causing a whirlpool. On the Creating river, eddies are circular movements of energy causing a lack of forward momentum as you swirl around and around in repeating familiar patterns.

> Eddies represent patterns; neither positive nor negative. Patterns are manifestations of lessons you need to learn. The lessons will be repeated over and over again until you change your response. Your attention and energy is required to stay afloat and keep your head above water while in the eddy. This increased attention is what allows you to learn your lesson. Similarly, in rivers, eddies are followed by places of still movement where minerals are deposited.

> When swirling in an eddy, an above-the-line question is, "What is the lesson here?"

> When swirling in an eddy, an under-the-line question is, "What is wrong here?" or "Why is this happening to me?" Never ask "why?" "Why?" requires you to make up a story to justify the reason that you are being shown a pattern. It invites judgment; criticism and blame; and rarely gives you an answer that will be useful to your forward momentum.

Navigational Tools

1. There is a colloquial definition of insanity, which is: repeating the same behavior over and over and expecting different results. An example would be repeatedly going into relationships with the same type of person and expecting a different result.

2. List any patterns that you can recognize and the lesson(s) they represent on the following chart.

PATTERN	LESSON

3. Pick one pattern you feel is the most detrimental to you. Create an action item or strategy to break the pattern. Write it below in the form of an intention, and be accountable to performing your action step.

PRINCIPLE 18 SHIFT YOUR ATTENTION

"If we have learned one thing from the history of invention and discovery, it is that in the long run—and often in the short one—the most daring prophecies seem laughably conservative."—Arthur C. Clarke, Science Fiction Author

Journey Notes

> Life is Plan B. If necessary, alter time and/or money to make your dream a reality.

> Never give up your dream. People who were interviewed about how they lived a life of self-actualization reported that they never lost sight of their dream. They continued to adjust their strategy by altering timing or financing (or both) until they were able to see their dream come true. Conclusion: Follow and stick to your dream.

Creating in Action

When Sheryl attended the Creating the Rest of Your Life™ workshop she was a long-time federal government employee with a good position and excellent benefits. However, her secret dream was to own her own business and be her own boss. In her government position, she had gained expertise in a specialized area of project procurement. She saw a business opportunity for someone to work outside of the government as a private contractor and to make a significant contribution to quality control. She wanted to be that someone. It was a perfect match for her dream.

During the workshop, she began to create a vision for this new venture and a strategy to exit her current job. She left the workshop with a one-year transition plan and a vision map in the form of a timeline. That was Plan A.

When Sheryl got into action, she found that there was an incredible amount of red tape involved in the process of licensing and bonding herself as a private government contractor. It was going to take longer than she had planned. *It was obvious that she would need a new plan. She had to alter both timing and money to make her dream a reality. That was Plan B.*

Even though she had to extend her launch date because of red tape, she never lost sight of her dream. While she was still salaried, she altered her Plan A financial strategy and allocated money to locate and train her team in advance of the launch. As Sheryl was interviewing for her team, she met and married her new life partner. It was a very happy surprise which made Plan B even more fulfilling.

By steadfastly holding to her vision, and altering time and money whenever necessary, Sheryl was able to bring her new business into being. In three years, she built her dream into a successful $6 million company. It went from Plan A vision and strategy with zero revenue, to Plan B launch and execution with millions in revenue within a three year period of time.

Navigational Tools

1. Draw a new version of your vision map in the form of a timeline; begin to put in dates and dollar estimates. This now becomes your strategy map. It may look like an artistic version of a spreadsheet.

2. Put your vision map and strategy map together; begin to create alignment between the two maps. Put this in a highly visible area and refer to it often.

PRINCIPLE 19 BECOME THE OBSERVER

"The real voyage of discovery consists not in seeking new landscapes, but in having new eyes."—Marcel Proust, Author and Social Critic

Journey Notes

> Staying curious and knowing nothing is the key to observing. The less you think you know about a person or situation, the more you remain open to all possibilities.

> The observer affects the outcome. Any preconceived ideas can alter how you see things and therefore the outcome.

> Analysis dulls intuition. If you stop analyzing (left brain) and start using your intuition (right brain) you access whole brain intelligence, thereby sharpening your observation skills.

Creating in Action

Linda was a partner in a five-person consulting firm in a metropolitan area. The firm was financially successful largely because she did the initial client interviews. She had a natural style and love of meeting people, and was a magnet for attracting new clients. Attraction marketing was her expertise. Her partners depended on her to do this, as well as consulting with the clients once they were enrolled.

However, after several years, Linda lost interest in her consultant role. During the Clarity process she was coached to pay attention and note whenever she felt energized in her work. *By staying curious and observing her energy, she noticed she was very lights-on whenever she was speaking in public and promoting entrepreneurs who had powerful visions.* She became very clear that she wanted to coach individuals with powerful visions to become entrepreneurs and launch their own businesses. She took a sabbatical from the firm and, fortunately, her partners supported the change.

When Linda left the partnership and became a soloist, there was a definite decline in her income. In reality, the decline was sharper than she had expected. And, as she was a 50% financial supporter of her family, the decline created stress at home. After six months, she realized that being on her own was not going to work out financially.

She returned to her position at the firm and immediately she was back in a familiar pattern, just like being in an eddy as represented by the Creating Journey Map. *Knowing that the observer affects the outcome, she dropped all preconceived ideas from her previous experience. She stayed open and curious, paying attention to her energy.*

Stepping back in was an easy transition, like doing the job "with her eyes closed." *By using her intuition and avoiding an urge to analyze the situation,* she realized that she was getting lulled back into old patterns. It was becoming increasingly harder for her to stay sharp and creative. Linda sensed that she was back in this pattern to learn a lesson about being true to herself.

After three months of swirling in that eddy and becoming progressively bored and drained, she shifted her attention to what "lit her up." She said to herself, "I'm okay. There's nothing seriously knocking me out here, but I am going to sleep and that is not okay. What I really want to do besides public speaking is write a book about brilliant enterprises. I want to honor this calling and be true to myself."

She resigned from the partnership and started writing. It was like kicking out of an eddy in a river; she felt stronger and wiser for the experience. Very soon thereafter, she and a partner formed a group to promote exciting entrepreneurial projects, and they started a new firm.

Presently, Linda is doing the public speaking for the firm and her book has been published. She has financial flow and is very lights-on.

Navigational Tools

1. Stay curious. Look at all people and situations as if they are brand new to you—a concept called "beginner's mind."

2. Utilize the ancient wisdom of the quote "...be in the world but not of it."

3. Gather resources, stay objective, and don't take any information personally. Note the lesson to be learned.

PRINCIPLE 20 EMBRACE THE EDDY

"Mistakes are lessons of wisdom. The past cannot be changed. The future is yet in your power."—Hugh White, President Pro Tempore of U.S. Senate, 1832

Journey Notes

Eddy—A circular movement of water causing a whirlpool, the swirling effect of which will impede your forward momentum. Remember that eddies represent patterns, therefore the energy will feel familiar, like "been here before, and done that." Eddies are normal and will be encountered frequently along your journey as you change and adjust your course. Learning to navigate the eddies is a vital component of the Creating journey.

> Lessons are learned by repeating patterns. Being sent back into a familiar pattern will give you an opportunity to experience it in a different way. It is similar to being given a test for pattern recognition.

> Practicing gratitude enhances ease and grace. If you are in an eddy revisiting a pattern, you will know that you haven't yet learned what you need to learn from that situation or person. In this awareness, be grateful because you may not have to repeat the lesson again. You can recognize the pattern; stop the process of being sent back and increase your forward momentum.

> When you kick out downstream of an eddy, you will be stronger and wiser for the experience. You will have learned to hold your vision, no matter what, and you will have new depth of experience.

> You release patterns that are no longer of service to you, first by recognizing the patterns (discovery), and second by shifting your

attention to your path (recovery). This process of rapid discovery and rapid recovery is essential to the success of your journey.

Creating in Action

Helen, a graphic designer, made the decision to leave her salaried position and start an entrepreneurial venture with her life partner. Together they created a home-based decorating product business, which they operated successfully for a year. It was a very creative time and they enjoyed working for themselves.

Helen had fun designing the packaging and creating the marketing connections while her partner designed and produced the design products. The business quickly became profitable. However, the fact that all of their income came from only one source began to cause Helen stress. To her, having a steady salary looked very appealing, and so she decided to return to work at a design studio.

Returning to graphic design, Helen had an opportunity to experience her work in a different way. She was in front of a computer for eight hours a day with no flexible time. She realized that it was knocking her lights out. Having a salary did not make up for the loss of creativity and freedom. She was learning a big lesson about what was really important to her. She stayed curious about it and watched for what she enjoyed.

Helen paid close attention to her energy as she worked at both her graphic design job and her entrepreneurial business. She discovered that she loved holding the visionary view of the whole design project and managing it through to completion.

She also realized she did not have the personality to be an entrepreneur and wanted to be part of a team in a larger organization. What she really wanted was to be an "intrapreneur." She and her partner decided to close their business, and Helen sought a position that contained all of the elements she enjoyed most.

She is now employed as operations manager with an on-demand, digital print and publishing company. This new position has provided increased in-

Part II—Principle 20 Embrace the Eddy

come and allows Helen to blend her technical and creative skills, while holding the visionary view for everyone on her team.

Helen was very grateful for the entrepreneurial experience and has instituted a team approach to the way her firm handles all of their large projects. Overall, there is a lot more ease, clients are served at a higher level, and Helen is enjoying being a part of a larger organization. *She is grateful for the ease and grace that came from the lessons and the experience of returning to her graphic design work.*

An additional lesson she learned, while swirling in the eddy, was that she did not have the personality for being an entrepreneur. Specifically, the uneven income stream and the uncertainty of client orders just didn't work for her. *When Helen kicked out downstream of her eddy, she became stronger and wiser for the experience. She learned to hold on to her vision, no matter what, and gained a deeper and richer understanding of her journey, including the value of her lessons.*

Navigational Tools

1. Reflect on the lessons you have learned on the Creating journey. Who are the people responsible for you learning your lessons? Write a sincere gratitude statement to each person.

PATTERN	LESSON

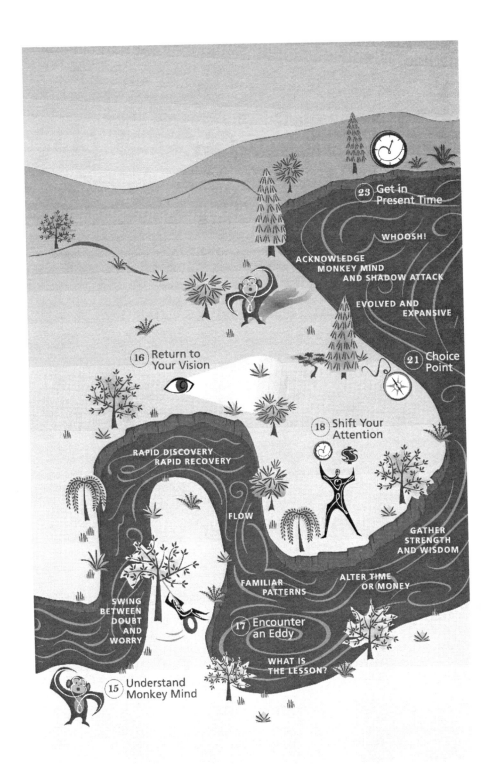

PRINCIPLE 21 CHOOSE WISELY— CHOICE POINT

"Revealing and realizing Noble Purpose is about returning to that which is most essential within you, discovering your perfect wisdom, fulfilling that which seeks expression within you. The journey to Noble Purpose is essentially awakening from your deep sleep to this inner call."—Dr. Barry Heermann, Author and Organizational Educator

Journey Notes

Choice Point—Divergent channels appear, which create an opportunity to explore different possibilities. Choice points occur moment by moment, like being at a crossroads and making a decision which way to turn. Learning to navigate choice points is an essential part of the Creating journey.

> Choice points compel you to use free will and make conscious decisions.
> Every decision you make is a result of having been at a choice point.
> Your choices create your reality.
> Choose lights-on passion and above the line action, rather than lights-off patterns and under the line drama.

Creating in Action

At age 57, Gary was at a major choice point. The decision he was facing would affect how he spent the rest of his life. He understood that his choice in this matter would create his reality and this made his process very intentional and thoughtful.

The choice point he was facing was finding a life partner, someone with whom he could connect on all levels—body, mind and spirit. He felt as if he had been searching his whole life for this elusive person, never finding exactly what he was looking for in partnership. He valued committed relationships and family ties. He had been married previously, and had a wonderful son. Still he was unfulfilled. After being divorced for several years, he had a deep desire to find his soul mate.

At this choice point he felt compelled to do things differently, by making conscious decisions during his search; breaking a pattern of compromise and inability to fully commit to a relationship. This time he was going to choose passion (lights-on) over pattern (lights-off), no matter what!

Of course, doubt and monkey mind entered the scene, which caused him to question if he really could do it differently this time. His pattern from previous relationships was to romanticize about a person, accept compromise and then feel guilty when the situation was unfulfilling. *Many of his past decisions at choice points were made when he lacked clarity about his life.*

After a few years of dating he realized some of the old patterns kept coming up. He made a **conscious decision** to stop dating for an extended period of time and instead spend the time gaining clarity. He hired a coach and began the process of refreshing his vision.

Navigational Tools

1. Listen to all input and make certain that you take responsibility for making your own choices.

PRINCIPLE 22 REFRESH YOUR VISION

"Heaven doesn't help the one who doesn't act."—Sophocles, Ancient Greek Playwright

Journey Notes

> The process of continuous refinement on the Creating journey accelerates an expanded and evolved vision.

> Accelerated flow is a result of your ability to strongly hold your personal field against detours, doubt, eddies and monkey mind.

> Exploring all of your "I wonder ifs" and putting them onto a vision map will increase the momentum, the "whoosh" effect, of your Creating journey.

Creating in Action

Gary arrived at a refreshed vision—it was both evolved and expansive. His coach assigned him to write down a description of an ideal partner—a profile of the woman he wanted in his life. He was very specific and very clear about the qualities of that person. Doubt and a lot of monkey mind had him wondering if he was the man who could attract the woman he described.

At his coach's urging, he drafted a profile of who he was and, in the process, more tightly defined the woman he was seeking. He created for himself a new, refreshed vision with a lot of detail and became very clear about what he wanted. *He put all of his "I wonder ifs" onto a vision map. It was a process of continuous refinement requiring him to look at who he was, as well as who he wanted to attract.*

Gary began dating again with a specific purpose in mind—finding his true life partner. During the next year he dated a number of interesting and amazing women. Staying committed to his vision, he didn't follow his previous pattern and settle for some very likely, but not exact, candidates. He shared his ideal profile with a close friend, who knew him well, and the friend started matchmaking. A few months later his friend introduced him to a woman who fit his profile precisely. Because *he held his personal field and didn't follow his old pattern of accepting less than he wanted or moving forward with a lack of clarity, flow was accelerated.*

A month after meeting her and knowing he had found his mate, they made the decision to get married. From choice point to making a conscious vision-supported decision, Gary got everything he wanted and experienced the *acceleration of the "whoosh" effect.*

Navigational Tools

1. Adjust your vision map to include any additions to your vision.

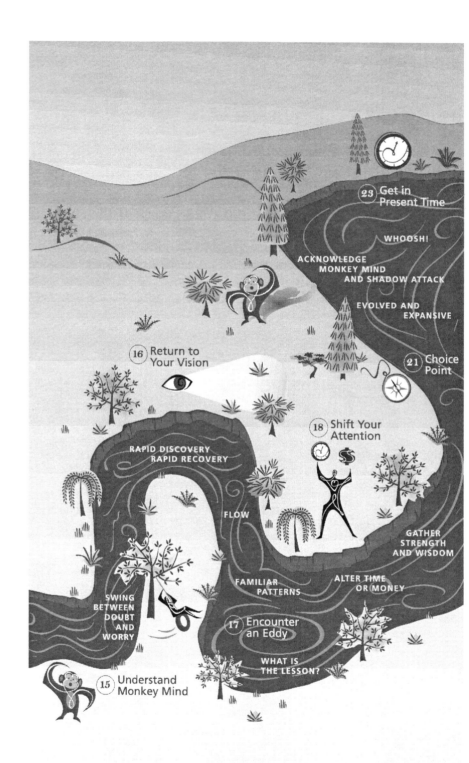

PRINCIPLE 23 GET IN PRESENT TIME

"Realize deeply that the present moment is all you ever have."—Eckhart Tolle, Contemporary Author

Journey Notes

> Asking the question, "What will it take right now to advance my vision?" will keep you in present time instead of in the past or future.

> Bridge Plan—a visioning process giving you a strategy to go from where you are in present time to where you want to go in the future, while remaining energized, clear and intentional.

> Shadow Talk is an internal conversation that makes up stories and limits your possibilities. It is melodramatic, draining, judgmental and critical.

> Acknowledging the presence of monkey mind and shadow talk shifts your attention from doubt and worry to your destiny.

> When you get clarity, you will see both your light and your shadow. You will be fully awake. Therefore, consciousness is not for sissies.

Creating in Action

When Sharon started the Creating the Rest of Your Life™ workshop, she was ready to reinvent her life. She was vibrantly healthy, in her early 50's, and had helped her two children through college. She was looking to the second half of her life as an open book, waiting for her to write the future.

Knowing she could do anything she wanted, any way that she wanted, she said, "This time it's for me! I am ready to do life my way." Yet, she wasn't clear about what that looked like. Paradoxically, she felt an exhilarating sense of freedom and, at the same time, she was totally baffled as to her direction.

Feeling stuck, she asked herself, *"What will it take right now to create the clarity that I need to advance my vision?"*

Sharon realized that she needed a bridge plan to keep her in action until she became crystal clear about her future. In present time, she had to address her ability to support herself while pursuing her dream, whatever that turned out to be. Her job at a large software company was her sole source of income. It was necessary for her to leverage her remaining time and salary and make them both serve her big picture. She had a deep faith that if she was clear about what she wanted and put that vision out into the universe, the universe would handle the details.

When Sharon was eighteen she had a dream to combine spiritual life with psychology and the arts. In the visioning process, she got clear about her future. She wanted to pursue her dream to go to college full time, study to be a spiritual psychologist, and relocate to a warmer climate. To make that happen as soon as possible, she needed to quit her job and absorb the consequences of leaving before she was fully vested in her employer's retirement plan.

Wanting to concentrate fully on her schooling meant she needed a plan allowing her to live without an income for several years. The company stocks were her only asset and their value was at an all time low. It seemed like an impossible dream. It wasn't penciling out for her, and *the monkey mind and shadow talk began an intense conversation saying that she was crazy to be dreaming like this! True to its melodramatic and critical nature, monkey mind and shadow talk made up a "worst case scenario," picturing her as a destitute bag lady.*

Fortunately, she was coached enough to recognize the presence of monkey mind and shadow talk. She shifted her attention from the doubt and worry of a "worst case scenario" to her destiny, which is the "best case scenario." This shift of attention broke the pattern where monkey mind and shadow talk had her going in circles and unable to go into action.

With her vision clear, Sharon started to gather information about programs for counseling and spiritual psychology. In addition to factual information, she also wanted to pay attention to clues and synchronicity. She called this being open to guidance. For her, following clues was really fun!

Since part of her vision was to live in a cottage in a warmer climate, she decided to investigate possibilities in a city she loved—Santa Fe, New Mexico. Within weeks, her sister called "out of the blue" offering Sharon a house sitting position, rent-free. It was very synchronous that her sister's rental house had just been vacated, and she wanted a trustworthy person to live in it who could supervise a remodel. It was located in southern California and it was on Santa Fe Street!

When Sharon put those clues together—free rent, a cottage located on Santa Fe Street, and a nearby university offering her desired program, she felt truly guided. She knew that the timing was right for her to go into action.

She has thoroughly enjoyed being able to live frugally, without an income, in a beautiful and warm place for the last two years while completing her education. She graduates soon and is already working with abused children using expressive arts.

Navigational Tools

1. Remove judgment and criticism by assessing your behavior using the method of "what worked" and "what didn't work." Don't make judgments of right or wrong, good or bad.

WHAT WORKED	WHAT DIDN'T WORK

2. Look for any patterns; do more of what worked and less of what didn't work.

PRINCIPLE 24 STAY AWAKE

"You'll see it when you believe it."—Dr. Wayne Dyer, Author and Spiritual Speaker

Journey Notes

> Messages appear every 5 – 7 seconds. These messages are either a lesson or a clue.

> You must be awake and aware to see the clues or learn the lesson.

> Synchronicity allows the clues to fit together into a bigger picture. Synchronicity means a coincidence of events that seem to be meaningfully related. At this point on the Creating journey, all clues point to your destiny. Begin to think of your destiny as a big jigsaw puzzle, as you sort through the clues. You discard all of the lights-off pieces involving log jams, doubt, monkey mind and shadow talk. All of the clues that remain in front of you are lights-on "destiny pieces" that link together, forming a clear picture to guide you forward.

Creating in Action

Having been laid off from her job at a photo lab, Tammy decided that it was time to get clear about her calling and find her "big IT." She needed something that she could pour herself into without doubt. She had one "big IT" clue from her childhood while playing on a classic flute and how that had stimulated in her a love of music. But, she had abandoned this thought as she grew up and went to work.

Fortuitously, the lay-off created an opening for her to attend a powerful transformational workshop and during that experience she awakened to her calling. She had a knowing at a deep cellular level that her destiny was to be a singer/songwriter and perform publicly before large audiences.

From that moment on, her energy was focused upon becoming a performer. The clues came rapidly and continuously. *All of these clues were destiny pieces that linked together and formed a clear picture guiding her forward.* Her challenge was to stay awake and aware, and to recognize the events and people as being part of her destiny.

Tammy remembered a clue that had appeared a year earlier when, for the first time in her life, she won something—an electric guitar! She had spent a few seconds to enter a drawing and then forgot about it until the call came saying that she had won. She started to play the guitar seriously and began writing songs for the first time since she was seventeen. More and more songs came and she had a physical sensation of waves rushing through her body, like an overwhelming feeling of gratitude. She was finally saying "yes!" to music, the thing that she wanted to do her whole life but didn't think she could.

Saying yes to her destiny led her to rent a small theater and put on the first "Tammy Show". Although she was very nervous about performing in front of an audience, she persisted and received a standing ovation. This led to more live performances. Her singing and song writing was attracting attention from local musicians, who believed in her music so much they worked with Tammy for free to produce a recording of her first seven songs.

Magic in the form of synchronicity continued to happen when she wanted to record her first full-length album. The budget to produce it was $17,000.00. It seemed like an impossible dream. Then, *"out of the blue"* her grandmother sent her $10,000.00! Simultaneously, a *message arrived* from a company that finds inheritances informing her there was an account in her name with $6,500.00 in it! She suddenly and unexpectedly had the $16,500.00 necessary to fund the next leg of her journey.

One of Tammy's favorite ways to earn money was to play at private parties. At one of these parties, on New Year's Eve, just three years after discovering her destiny, she was heard by a couple who loved to invest in up and coming artists. *These investors gave her yet another clue to her destiny, as well as a whole new venue to make money doing what she loved, when they asked her to give them voice lessons. This launched her into a career as a voice coach.*

This style of performing and coaching has supported her while she married, had a daughter, endured a divorce and continued onward into her lights-on life as a mother and performer.

Synchronicity continues to fit the clues together into a bigger picture as she pursues her music career. When Tammy plays, people are mesmerized by her music. As she looks at the lights in the eyes of the audience, she is heart-connected to the truth of her calling. She has perfected her songwriting and singing, and has 30 great songs to choose from when her new CD is produced.

Navigational Tools

LIST ALL CLUES

_____

_____

_____

_____

_____

_____

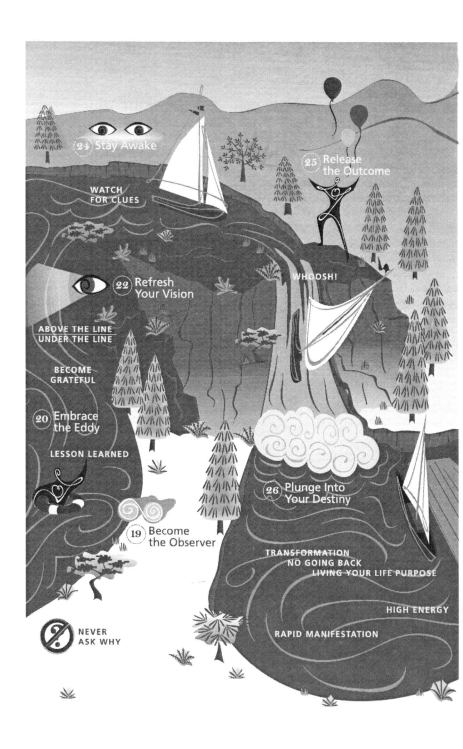

PRINCIPLE 25 RELEASE THE OUTCOME

"You must give birth to your images. They are the future waiting to be born. Fear not the strangeness that you feel. The future must enter you long before it happens. Just wait for the hour, the birth of new clarity."—Ranier Maria Rilke, German Poet

Journey Notes

> There is a formula for manifestation.

  Intention + Attention + Action + Release = manifestation of your vision.

> Vision to action occurs rapidly. In Creating terms, this is known as the "whoosh effect", which denotes a very short time gap between envisioning an outcome and when it actually occurs. In some cases, this can be instantaneous. Therefore, fasten your seat belt and be very clear about what you ask for.

> Everything is perfect, and as it should be. Sometimes what initially shows up may not look perfect to you at the time. However, by successfully releasing the outcome, which is your willful picture of how you think it should look, you allow the opportunity of serendipity to provide your perfect solution. When you release your attachment to the outcome you can say, "I was clear about my intention and what showed up is perfect."

Creating in Action

Gerri has a very successful business selling real estate. Her success is a direct result of the individual attention and time she spends with each client, because she loves her work. More expansive than the role of a real estate agent, she helps people find their ideal living space and smoothly handles all of the details to make their dreams come true. Her clients love her and she has made deep friendships with many of them.

In addition to real estate matchmaking, she has another love, which she discovered during a shamanic retreat—protecting the endangered sea turtles. From the moment of discovery, making an impact on the plight of the sea turtles has become her calling. Her deep desire is to give a gift to the planet, using her time and real estate profits, by establishing a sea turtle sanctuary on an island somewhere in the Caribbean. Gerri's vision is that the property would contain both the sanctuary and a retreat center for eco-tourism.

To accomplish this, she and her husband took a sabbatical and traveled throughout the Caribbean on a sailboat. They specifically chose the sailboat process to look for the island, because it would mimic the same vantage point that a turtle would use when looking for a place to land and lay eggs. The trip proved to be magical! Many sea turtles came right up to the boat and showed themselves. Gerri came to believe that the turtle was her totem, her spirit guide from the animal kingdom. One turtle in particular was huge, and the captain said it was the largest, and therefore the oldest, turtle he had seen in all his years sailing those waters.

During the weeks of their sailing, they stopped at several ports and investigated available real estate. They explored a lot and had fun but nothing appeared to meet her vision. *Fortunately, Gerri's belief system that "everything is perfect" kept them from being discouraged. They released their original intention that this trip would result in a purchase* and returned home knowing more time and money would be necessary to find the right island property.

To raise more money for the turtle sanctuary, Gerri became very intentional about manifesting a new real estate project capable of rapidly producing income. Setting her intention for a project to present itself, she put her attention on calling all of her developer contacts. This action was successful and, within weeks, she landed a contract to sell 102 new homes. She accepted the contract and sold out the whole project within 3 months! She was very clear about what she asked for and it manifested.

Gerri's search for the perfect Caribbean location continues. She proved the principle that *vision to action occurs rapidly.*

Navigational Tools

1. Notice how quickly your clues manifest. Often, it happens as quickly as you think it. Example: You think of someone, the phone rings, and it is them.
2. Write down some examples of synchronous events in your life.

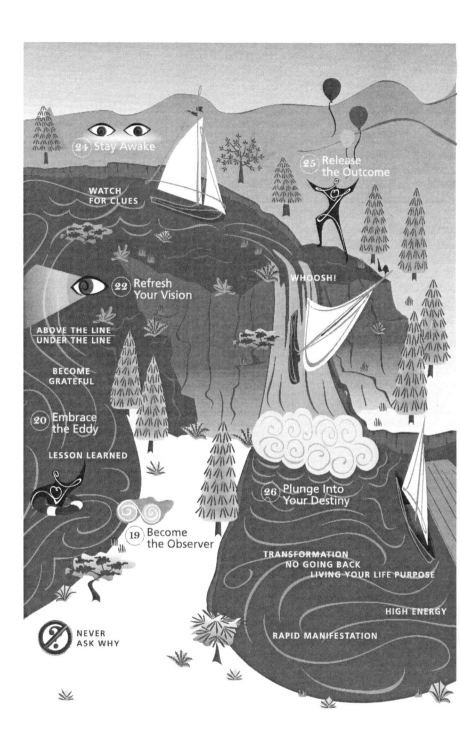

PRINCIPLE 26 PLUNGE INTO YOUR DESTINY

"You are what your deep driving desire is. As your desire is, so is your will. As your will is, so is your deed. As your deed is, so is your destiny."—Upanishads, Ancient Mystical Teachings

Journey Notes

> A central theme clearly describing your life purpose has emerged from all of the previous visions. There is a radical increase in your energy. You are able to understand your own distinct energy patterns and how to stay lights-on. At this point, manifestation is extremely rapid. You envision and your vision shows up. You know that you are following guidance instead of your will.

> There is a cellular learning of your destiny through a heart connection to your vision. This is termed the heart-mind when you have a knowing of your passion. You no longer have to refer to your notes when people ask you what you are passionate about. You are lights-on and doing what you love most of the time. There is no going back and doing your life the old way.

> Analyzing no longer serves you. Old thinking patterns have dissolved. Analyzing and thinking your way through decisions is a pattern of the past. You recognize that what you create is intentional. There are no accidents and, therefore...

> Life is good. Even when difficult life events like divorce and getting fired occur, you will appreciate the opportunity they present for learning and growth. Earlier in the Creating journey you would have thought of these events as catastrophic. However, you now recognize the perfection and synchronicity and can focus on

gratitude for the lessons you have learned. This is the place where, 100% of the time, you will recognize that "life is good."

Navigational Tools

1. Have a picture taken of yourself. Look at it objectively as if you don't know who it is. Look for overall balance, vitality and lights-on appearance.

2. Write down the central theme that has emerged for your life. From your prior visioning, the "what" has merged with the "how-to," they are one and the same.

PRINCIPLE 27 LIVE LIGHTS-ON!

"Unless you leave room for serendipity, how can the divine enter? The beginning of the adventure of finding yourself is to lose your way."—Joseph Campbell, Author and Professor

Journey Notes

> Transformation has occurred. You are living a full life. You are able to equally value both the peaks and the valleys.

> Rapid discovery and rapid recovery are fully functioning. Although catastrophic life events occur, (people and pets may die, accidents may happen), you are able to stay on your path and continue after appropriate grieving. You are able to experience the grief process and release it. You will see that obstacles are opportunities to be creative and grow. You value and respect the lessons you learn.

> Energy remains constant. You feel that your path is one of service; you are responding to guidance; you are following energy with your lights-on; and overall, your life experiences calibrate at 9.5 and above.

> Tremendous value is placed on everything that you have encountered on your life journey.

Creating in Action

Cathy has arrived at this place on her journey, and speaks of her life now as a series of peak experiences with some occasional valley moments. As she stands on the peak looking back on the river that she has navigated, the river looks small. Yet she acknowledges that at the beginning of the journey the river looked huge, and many of the obstacles looked impassable. Her perspective has changed completely from one of effort and drama to one of ease and grace, because she learned the lessons and practices the Clarity principles daily.

Cathy started her journey in 1994 when she retired from a 28 year career in periodontal dental hygiene. It had been a very good career. She was happily married, made plenty of money and totally enjoyed being a mother to her son.

Life was good, but eventually she lost her passion for her work. She started asking, "What's next? What do I want to do that has meaning and purpose, and kindles my passion?" She read books, listened to tapes, went to seminars and couldn't get an answer to *what* to do. She got lots of *how* to do answers, but nothing about *what*—nothing about passion.

She knew that a different approach was being called for and summoned up her courage to quit her financially-secure profession. With a giant leap of faith into the unknown, she went on sabbatical to learn new things and to explore her destiny.

During the course of her 18-month sabbatical, she studied with several well- known teachers who were working with the concepts of passion and purpose. It was a wonderful time of exploring; *she refined her focus* to learning everything she could about the **distinctions** between passion, energy and life purpose.

During her studies, Cathy realized that a huge gap existed between the theory of passion and a practice to discover passion. Highly curious by nature, she kept studying and having fun learning new concepts. This was very energizing. She looked and felt years younger, like a new person from the inside out.

By the end of the sabbatical, she was so noticeably radiant that people started to ask her what she was doing differently and whether they could be guided to achieve similar results. This gave Cathy the clue for a whole new career—coaching others to find their vision and vitality. *Practicing sacred self-ishness,* Cathy finished her studies and *designed her vision.*

She had accumulated a wealth of knowledge, which she synthesized into the Lights On Learning Method™ of interviewing, and launched into her second career.

Clients showed up immediately. Cathy noticed that she was attracting clients interested in entrepreneurial visions but not attracting corporate clients. Their not showing up was a sure clue that the corporate types would have created *resistance* to her new methodology.

A clear flow pattern was emerging and Cathy followed the energy of the flow. The more adept Cathy got about this process of following energy and staying in flow, the more it felt like she was being carried by a river and the clear image of a winding river kept appearing to her.

This image got stronger and stronger. She saw it in her mind's eye every time she coached someone. While they were talking she could visualize where they were and where they needed to go next. She felt that she was being shown the river as a metaphor to guide others to find their way. Cathy got clear and *intentional* that her calling was to make a river image into an easy-to-use tool for people when they felt lost. She started by sketching what she saw and sharing the sketch with her clients. They loved it and wanted a river map and guide book of their own.

These requests put her at a *choice point* in her journey. She needed to decide if she was going to venture into the world of publishing and add that to her already busy workshop-style coaching practice. Her future would be molded by the decision she made at this choice point.

Following her own energy, and realizing that she was passionate about teaching the river principles, she *created a new vision* to include writing, teaching, speaking and coaching. In addition, she *initiated that vision* by hiring a graphic designer to turn the rough sketch into an artistic map.

As Cathy went into flow as an author, she encountered some big challenges. The next leg of her journey looked and felt like "a dark night of the soul." Her husband was not supportive of her new direction and presented some difficult ultimatums.

She faced the biggest *choice point* of her life. Was she going to stay in a marriage which had a lot of history but no longer had love, respect and support? A divorce looked imminent. This was a dilemma which required deep reflection regarding choosing passion over pattern.

She *detoured* for several months, took a time-out for coaching and counseling, and got back into flow, returning to her vision to be the author of the Creating Atlas, and creator of the Creating Journey Map.

This is when *doubt* entered. Cathy had to face her fears. After 28 years of marriage, could she make it on her own? Could she hire a new team and run her business by herself? Would she ever find a partner to love completely, or would she spend the rest of her life alone? And how about writing a book for the first time? Who was she to think she could write something that people would want to read? *Monkey mind* chattered incessantly and had her swinging between doubt and worry. Luckily, her vision was so compelling that she got back into action with writing and teaching to keep her lights-on.

Ending her long-term marriage was difficult, and Cathy tried to make it work one more time. It was quickly evident, when *encountering that eddy,* that divorce remained the most compassionate solution. When they tried to be together again, there was clearly no passion left. It was time for them to part as friends and to go their separate ways. This required Cathy to *shift her attention* from writing, move from her home of 30 years, get her son into a new school and get grounded. This was a major upheaval!

Becoming an observer of everything that was happening, instead of taking things personally, was one of the most challenging parts of Cathy's journey thus far. The saving grace was her decision to go to gratitude; *embrace the eddies* for all the lessons they had taught her; and create value from the strength and wisdom she had gained.

Two years later, the next *choice point* presented itself when a friend and colleague said that he wanted to introduce Cathy to a man who could potentially be her life partner. The decision to even be willing to meet this person was a huge defining moment. She ignored monkey mind, *got in present time,* and decided to *stay wide awake* to the fact that her friend knew her very well and also knew him very well. There are no accidents, and this was not a "blind" date. This was an intentional and thoughtful matchmaking event.

Cathy trusted the situation, initially connecting with him through phone and email, and then accepted an invitation to meet him at the home of their matchmaking friends. As soon as she made that decision, she *released the outcome* and flew to meet Gary. *It was this event that caused her to plunge into her destiny…to love, work and create within the framework of a spiritual partnership.*

Within moments of being in each other's physical presence, it was clear to both of them that they were destined to be together. They simultaneously experienced a deep awareness that responding to guidance and following energy clues had resulted in them finding one another. Fortuitously, they have a shared vision and compatible paths of service. Cathy and Gary have married and merged their personal and professional lives, modeling a co-creative partnership—*definitely 9.5 and above!*

PRINCIPLE 28 THANK GOD IT'S MONDAY!

"Too much of a good thing is just right."—Mae West, Actress and Humorist

The dream of *living* the life you want *and loving* what you do is alive and absolutely attainable.

We know this can be your new reality. In this book we have shared stories of clients who have used the Creating principles and strategies to create a new reality for themselves based on their individual lights-on vision.

People, like you, who are:

> Living each day happily free from judgment or criticism.
> Creating a new reality by making daily choices that are lights-on.
> Choosing only energizing actions to move them toward their vision.
> Attracting what they want into their life effortlessly.
> Focusing on and manifesting magnificent lives.

The present social system advocates and reinforces struggle and effort as the methodology to get what you want in order to achieve success. It reinforces the "life is hard, get over it" mentality. This mentality promotes exhausting oneself, and the resulting tiredness manifests itself universally in many unhealthy ways.

For example, we've read that human beings are the only mammals on earth that have heart attacks specifically on Monday mornings. Another cultural example is the "Thank God It's Friday" mentality and the accompanying lifestyle of dragging through the work week, living for the weekends and dreading Monday mornings. This continues on through the working years, which translates into waiting for retirement, or better yet early retirement, to live your life fully.

When you embark on this "loving what you do and doing what you love" lifestyle, you will notice how contrary your actions are to the cultural norm that is prevalent today. That is the good news. Your lights-on life will be very different, and very vibrant.

No matter how you choose to define it, the dream of living the life you want and loving what you do will continue to thrive. Keeping the dream alive is very simple if you just take the time to apply the strategies you've learned in this Creating Atlas. Return often to the journey notes and the navigational tools to keep living your inspired vision.

This Creating Atlas has introduced you to some simple, yet very powerful, concepts. You now have an inspired vision of what you want your life and work to look like. You will use this knowledge and these tools for the rest of your life—to find your next new vision, to course-correct on your way to your destiny, to enhance your relationships and to bring more joy and vitality into each and every day. Lights ARE an inside job, and you know how to turn them on.

We named this principle *Thank God It's Monday!* because we believe everyone can go to work every day and feel excited. We know you can wake up every morning and spend the day doing the work you love. We know that all of your relationships can be energetic and effortless. And, we believe you can fully live each day of your life with vitality, energy and passion!

We know it is possible for ordinary people to live extraordinary lives.

REFERENCES AND SUGGESTED READING

Arrien, Angeles. Signs of Life—The Five Universal Shapes and How to Use Them. New York: Tarcher / Putnam, 1992

Briggs, John and Peat, David. Seven Lessons of Chaos—Spiritual Wisdom From the Science of Change. New York: Harper Collins, 1999

Braden, Gregg. The Isiah Effect—Decoding the Lost Science of Prayer and Prophecy. New York: Three Rivers Press, 2000

Campbell, Joseph. The Power of Myth. New York: Anchor Books, 1991

Chopra, Deepak. How to Know God—The Soul's Journey Into the Mystery of Mysteries. New York: Harmony Books, 2000

Collinge, William. Subtle Energy—Awakening to the Unseen Forces in Our Lives. New York: Warner Books, 1998

Csikszentmihalyi, Mihaly. Flow—The Psychology of Optimal Experience. New York: Harper & Row, 1990

Dyer, Dr. Wayne W. The Power of Intention. California: Hay House, 2004

Hawkins, David R. Power VS Force—The Hidden Determinates of Human Behavior. California: Hay House, 1995

Heerman, Barry. Noble Purpose. Virginia: QSU Publishing, 2004

Holmes, Ernest. The Science of Mind. New York: Tarcher / Putnam, 1998

LeVoy, Gregg. Callings—Finding and Following and Authentic Life. New York: Harmony Books, 1997

Luhrs, Janet. The Simple Living Guide. New York: Broadway Books, 1997

McTaggart, Lynne. The Field—The Quest for the Secret Force of the Universe. New York: Harper Collins, 2002

Myss, Caroline. Anatomy of the Spirit. New York: Harmony Books, 1996

Myss, Caroline. Sacred Contracts—Awakening Your Divine Potential. New York: Harmony Books, 2001

Redfield, James. The Secret of Shambala—In Search of the Eleventh Insight. New York: Warner Books, 1999

Toms, Michael and Justine Willis. True Work—The Sacred Dimension of Earning a Living. New York: Bell Tower, 1998

THE AUTHORS

Joining forces to bring over 30 years of combined coaching expertise into this book, Cathy and Gary Hawk provide a proven process to transform the way people live and lead.

Cathy Hawk, veteran energy coach is Founding Partner of Clarity International™, a coaching firm specializing in the development of personal and professional vision. Cathy is a pioneer in the field of energy coaching and has the first trademarked interview system based on chakras. Using her innovative interview and image feedback process called **Lights on Learning Method™,** clients see their own energy with stunning clarity. As a result, they rapidly connect to their passion, look younger, feel energized, and quickly go into intentional action.

Since 1994, Cathy, along with Clarity-trained coaches, has inspired thousands of people from all walks of life to find and answer their callings, using energy as a primary life and work strategy. Drawing upon entrepreneurial expertise gathered from almost 30 years of visioning and team building in her professional practice, she has coached visionary entrepreneurs and business owners throughout the U.S. and Canada, to create enlightened business practices. She is a frequent guest on the acclaimed NPR program, New Dimensions.

Gary Hawk is Managing Partner of Clarity International™. Gary serves as an executive coach and mentor for CEOs, business owners and senior executives. He guides and challenges his clients in clarifying business and personal goals, and in thinking through the ongoing means to attain them. The focus of his work is primarily on increasing the ability of each client to be an authentic leader of self and others, and developing a clarity of purpose and the methods to achieve it.

With over 40 years experience in both large and small businesses, Gary brings a rich business background to his mentoring relationships. Since 1994, Gary has facilitated peer groups for CEOs and business owners. His peer groups provide a safe harbor for business owners to discuss the sensitive issues and challenges of leading and running a business.

CLARITY INTERNATIONAL®

The dream of living the life you want, and loving what you do is here waiting for you. All you have to do is call us and attend one of our workshops. Clarity International® provides personalized, easy-to-use, vision-based programs, strategies and tools to help visionary business leaders and individuals discover, design and implement what's next in their lives. The distinctive benefit of Clarity programs is the originality of our approach, combined with real importance in the value systems of our clients to find and create new meaning both in the world and in their personal lives.

Creating the Rest of Your Life™, is a pinnacle course for personal and professional excellence. It is a profound journey of self-knowledge and action designed to align your personal purpose with new thought, new meaning and expression of your individual passion.

Powerful Partnering™ retreats for business or life partners transform the way you work together. Moving from power struggles to co-creative adventures you create powerful movement to the next level of shared vision, trust and achievement.

Our programs are for you, if:

> You are genuinely looking for something better, and want to make an impact through your own unique expression of yourself.

> You are a visionary business leader and want to create a renewed vision and bringing increased purpose and energy to your work.

> You are asking yourself, "What's my purpose? How do I live my life fully?"

> You want more passion, vitality and energy in your life and work.

> You no longer want to be an accidental tourist in your own life.

> You want an answer to "what lights me up?"

To find out more, contact us at:

clarityinternational@clarityinternational.com or toll-free *877.335.9333.*

To purchase a full color version of the Creating the Rest of Your Life Journey Map go to *www.clarityinternational.com.*

A thank you to our readers: In appreciation for reading *Creating the Rest of Your Life*, we will send you an audio CD of a thought provoking interview where Cathy Hawk discusses many of the Clarity principles. To request your CD, contact clarityinternational@clarityinternational.com with your name and mailing address.

Clarity International®

www.clarityinternational.com

clarityinternational@clarityinternational.com

877.335.9333